Biomedical
Aspects
of
Depression

Biomedical Aspects of Depression

And Its Treatment

Ross J. Baldessarini, M.D., FAPA

Professor of Psychiatry   Harvard Medical School
Associate Director   Mailman Laboratories
for Psychiatric Research

American
Psychiatric
Press, Inc.

Portions of this book adapted from material previously published in the *McLean Hospital Journal*.

Library of Congress Cataloging in Publication data
Main entry under title:
Baldessarini, Ross J., 1937–
    Biomedical aspects of depression and its treatment

    Bibliography: p.
        1. Depression, Mental—Physiological aspects.
2. Depression, Mental—Chemotherapy.   3. Antidepressants.
I. Title. [DNLM: 1. Affective disorders—Psychotic.
2. Antidepressive agents—Pharmacodynamics. WM 207
B176b]
RC537.B335   1982   616.85'27   82-22659
Printed in the U.S.A.
ISBN 0–88048–004–1

For Deedee and Polly

...The body thus possessed with the unchearefull, and discomfortable darknes of melancholie, obscureth the Sonne and Moone, and all the comfortable planetts of our natures, in such sort, that if they appeare, they appeare all darke, and more then halfe eclipsed of this mist of blackenes, rising from that hideous lake...This affecting of the minde [by the body], J understand not to be any empairing of the nature thereof; or decay of any facultie therein...This effect as it is wrought by that kinde of disorder, in like manner, a perturbation whereon reason sitteth not and holdeth not raine, is of the same aptnes to disturbe the goodly order disposed by iust proportion in our bodies: & putting the parts of that most consonant and pleasant harmony out of tune deliver a note, to the great discontentment of reason and much against the mindes will, which intendeth far other, then the corporall instrument effecteth...The perturbations of melancholie are for the most parte, sadde and fearefull, and such as rise of them: as distrust, doubt, diffidence, or dispaire, sometimes furious, and sometimes merry in appearance...That melancholick humour...counterfetteth terrible objects to the fantasie, and polluting both the substance, and spirits of the brayne, causeth it without externall occasion to forge monstrous fictions...

Timothy Bright, *A Treatise on Melancholie*
T. Vautrollier; London, 1586

CONTENTS

1

GENERAL INTRODUCTION

2

THE BIOLOGY OF DEPRESSIVE DISORDERS

CONTENTS

3
RECENT ADVANCES IN
ANTIDEPRESSANT PHARMACOLOGY 85

4
SUMMARY AND CONCLUSIONS 127

LIST OF TABLES

LIST OF FIGURES

ACKNOWLEDGMENTS

This work was supported in part by a National Institute of Mental Health Research Career Award (MH-47370). The manuscript was prepared by Mrs. Mila Cason. Valuable consultations and reviews of preliminary manuscripts were provided by Bernard Carroll, M.D., Ray Fuller, PhD, Alan Gelenberg, M.D., and Bruce Lydiard, M.D., PhD.

PREFACE

This monograph documents a new movement and vitality in the biomedical study of depressions that promise to advance this crucial aspect of modern psychiatry. In recent decades, biomedical approaches in psychiatry have struggled for a legitimate place, especially at the level of clinical practice. Hypotheses of the biological causation of depression have remained little more than interesting and provocative speculations without impressive experimental support. While it is true that modern psychopharmaceutical treatments of depression and of manic-depressive illness have been clinically revolutionary, these treatments have been limited in efficacy and far from perfect in their safety. Moreover, our understanding of their mechanisms of action had virtually ended at the short-term effects that tend to potentiate the actions of monoamine synaptic neurotransmitters—effects well known since the 1960s.

While preparing a series of review papers for the *McLean Hospital Journal* and the *Directions in Psychiatry* series and in preparation for a second edition of my monograph *Chemotherapy in Psychiatry*, I was struck by several trends that strongly suggest an important new phase in the field. Among these trends are an increasing basis for skepticism regarding amine-based hypotheses of the pathophysiology of manic-depressive illness, a growing tendency to accept descriptive studies of depressed patients as a legitimate and worthy enterprise, and movement out of the rut of rediscovering imipramine-like antidepressants and of excessive emphasis on the blockade of amine reuptake as a crucial action mechanism of heterocyclic (imipramine-like) antidepressants.

I undertook this monograph to provide an overview of these rapid advances and shifts of emphasis in the biomedically oriented study of depression. This monograph also offers a more general opportunity to evaluate the impact and potential usefulness of biomedical psychiatry. Although portions of the material are available elsewhere, I hope that the present summary may help to clarify some themes and to provoke further critical discussions at a time when psychiatry, particularly biomedical and research psychiatry, is under unprecedented scrutiny by medical colleagues, by other nonmedical health professionals, by government regulatory and funding agencies, by insurance providers, by the legal profession and the courts, and by the general public.

The present monograph is *not* a comprehensive review of manic-depressive illness. It does not cover many clinical, diagnostic, psychological, therapeutic, and management issues. Even the biomedical and pharmacological topics that are covered are not dealt with exhaustively; instead, I have attempted to provide summaries and overviews with which to convey general trends in the field. Additional material is available in the reviews and monographs listed in the References.

Ross J. Baldessarini, M.D.
BOSTON, MASSACHUSETTS
April, 1982

1

General Introduction

THE NATURE OF BIOMEDICAL PSYCHIATRY

Biomedical psychiatry has traditionally been associated with the search for additional conditions to be turned over to colleagues in internal medicine or neurology (general paresis, the epilepsies, encephalitides, thyroid diseases, steroid psychoses, avitaminoses such as pellagra, and rare inborn errors of metabolism such as phenylketonuria). Each generation of medical investigators applied the newest technologies to search for causes of the remaining major mental illnesses of unknown etiology—notably schizophrenia, severe depression, and manic-depressive illness. There were waves of enthusiasm for studies of neuropathology, intermediary metabolism, immunology, and so forth. For the most part, these approaches have not been successful.

In addition, biomedical psychiatrists had acquired a reputation for being psychologically naïve, clinically insensitive, or even brutal in their applications of such experimental treatments as lobotomy and shock therapies. This reputation was especially strong in the face of extraordinary American optimism and enthusiasm for psychological hypotheses and

1

therapies, especially those arising from the psychoanalytic tradition. Alternative approaches of great theoretical (and some clinical) interest, arising from the disciplines of experimental psychology, have never quite caught hold in this country.

In the early 1950s a change began that continues to have a revolutionary impact on current theory and practice. This change included the introduction of antipsychotic, mood-altering, and antianxiety chemicals of indubitable efficacy, reasonable safety, and overwhelming clinical popularity and commercial success. Simultaneously, there were administrative, financial, and governmental changes that led to the community mental health movement and the phasing down of large and remote locked public mental institutions. These two movements appear to have interacted to result in the current office-based or community-hospital-based practice of most psychiatrists.

Along with the new psychopharmaceuticals developed a generation of pharmacologically oriented laboratory and clinical researchers who now have a dominant impact on clinical, as well as research, psychiatry. Many of their ideas have grown from a partial understanding of the actions of drugs upon the brain. Some of these ideas are intriguing and heuristic, but they are not without intellectual and practical risks. For example, it is commonly assumed that, if a drug can modify a psychiatric syndrome for better or worse, then that syndrome must have a biological basis to which the drug's actions are directly related. This view is even more attractive in light of suggestions of a genetic contribution to these syndromes. More specifically, if antidepressants enhance monoamine-mediated synaptic neurotransmission, or if antipsychotic agents block dopamine receptors, then it may follow that depression results from a deficiency of monoamine function, or that psychosis results from overactivity of dopamine systems in the forebrain. Nevertheless, this thesis may be as illogical as it would be to study the action mechanisms of thiazide diuretics in search of the cause of edema. The striking paucity of direct support for these hypotheses from a large body of clinical metabolic experimentation reinforces the point.

Another problematic aspect of psychopharmacologic theory is that partial understanding of the actions of antipsychotic and mood-altering agents may have biased or impeded the development of better new agents. Thus, virtually all currently available neuroleptics are antidopamine agents, which have similar limitations and neurological side effects as chlorpromazine, and nearly all available antidepressants antagonize the inactivation of norepinephrine. This result is not surprising, since pharmaceutical laboratories have been heavily influenced by these actions of old drugs in their search for new agents. Fortunately, this trend is changing. Thanks to a series of serendipitous clinical observations, there are now available, or soon to be released, a series of "atypical" antidepressants that do not have norepinephrine-potentiating actions or the toxicity of imipramine-like drugs; there are also experimental antipsychotic and antimanic agents that have only weak effects on dopamine systems and little neurological toxicity.

In clinical research, the biomedical approach is entering an important new phase that is fundamentally less theoretical and more clinical. For example, this more descriptive approach has led to the development and clinical use of the dexamethasone test and other endocrinologic and metabolic measurements in depression, firm findings of early onset of REM sleep in depression, the application of pharmacokinetic principles to drug therapy, and a descriptive approach to differential diagnosis exemplified by the current *Diagnostic and Statistical Manual* of the American Psychiatric Association (1).

It may be a sign of greater maturity and self-confidence in the field that biomedical researchers and clinicians can work more independently of pharmacologically based hypotheses and can more directly attempt to define and describe the conditions under study. Theory is fine to organize observations and plan the next experiments, and it can help to sell a research grant proposal. It can also be overdone or oversold; when research and observation are done in the service of theory, problems can arise. The newer, less theoretical, and more clinical approach is very encouraging and is starting to bear impressive practical fruit.

BIOMEDICAL ASPECTS OF DEPRESSION AND ITS TREATMENT

Research on the severe mood disorders provides the best example of current biomedical approaches in psychiatry. Depression is the most common serious psychiatric disorder. It leads to high rates of morbidity and incalculable economic losses, and it can be fatal. The lifetime risk of clinically significant depression is greater than one in ten.

The theory and management of manic and depressive illnesses (conditions marked by depression alone or by alternating elations or excited states and severe depressions) have virtually been revolutionized since the development of modern psychopharmacology in the 1950s. There has been a recent upsurge of interest in developing new antidepressant compounds and in understanding the actions of older drugs. Theories concerning the pathophysiology of manic and depressive illnesses have in the past been dominated by a partial understanding of drug actions. The resulting hypotheses have typically included suggestions that the functions of synaptic neurotransmitters (notably norepinephrine, serotonin, or other monoamines) may be deficient in depression and excessive in mania. Many attempts have been made to provide support for such proposals in direct clinical metabolic studies of depressed patients, and an overview of many of these is provided below.

A more recent development, however, has been to move beyond the testing of hypotheses based on the actions of mood-altering agents and to define and describe the clinical syndromes of depression and manic-depressive illness. This approach to mood disorders is providing strong support for the existence of unipolar and bipolar forms of depressive illnesses. It is also beginning to provide sound medical diagnostic tests for depression that may approach the reliability of those used in general medicine. The improvements in descriptive and clinical diagnosis are, in turn, leading to unprecedented improvement in clinical management of depressed patients.

At the same time, there have been important recent advances in understanding the actions of antidepressant treatments that have been available since the 1950s, as well as the introduction of novel agents. While most of the familiar antidepressants have been remarkably similar pharmacologically, several new "atypical" antidepressants (such as the recently released trazodone) promise to provide clinical benefits without enhancing the actions of monoamine neurotransmitters in conventionally understood ways, and they appear to be free of many of the toxic side effects of earlier agents.

It is now appropriate to take stock of these recent advances and to appraise the accomplishments and limitations of the biomedical approach to the depressions, since this provides an excellent example of the biomedical approach to modern psychiatric research and practice in general.

2
The Biology of Depressive Disorders

BACKGROUND

Historical Background

The severe disorders of mood or affect are among the most common of the major psychiatric syndromes (see Table 1). Lifetime expectancy or risk rates for such disorders are nearly 12% in the general population (2 5). Only a minority are treated by psychiatrists or in psychiatric hospitals, and about 70% of prescriptions for antidepressants are written by nonpsychiatrist physicians (6). These and other modern medical treatments of severe mood disorders have contributed to a virtual revolution in the theory and practice of modern psychiatry since the introduction of mood-altering drugs three decades ago (6–9). These agents include lithium salts (1949), the antimanic and antipsychotic (neuroleptic) agents such as chlorpromazine (1952), the monoamine oxidase (MAO) inhibitors (1952), and the tricyclic (imipramine-like) antidepressant agents (1957) (8). In addition, electroconvulsive therapy (ECT) continues to have a place in the treatment of very severe and acute mood disorders, especially life-threatening forms of depression (10).

The development of these modern medical therapies has had several important effects. First, these agents have provided relatively simple, specific, effective, and safe forms of treatment that have had a profound impact on current patterns of medical practice. For example, many depressed or hypomanic patients can be managed adequately in outpatient facilities, so that prolonged, expensive, and disruptive hospitalizations can be avoided. Second, partial understanding of the pharmacology of the new psychotropic drugs has led to imaginative hypotheses concerning the pathophysiology or etiology of severe mood disorders. These, in turn,

TABLE 1

Summary of Epidemiologic Data in Depressive Disorders

Category	N [a]	Mean Value ± SEM [b]
Nonbipolar (unipolar) depression		
Yearly incidence (%)	12	1.39 ± 0.76
Point prevalence (%)	16	5.27 ± 1.16
Yearly prevalence (%)	12	2.70 ± 1.29
Lifetime risk (%)	6	11.70 ± 2.40
Female:male sex ratio	21	2.00 ± 0.14
Bipolar (manic-depressive) illness		
Yearly incidence (%)	9	0.011 ± 0.002
Lifetime risk (%)	5	0.62 ± 0.11
Female:male sex ratio	6	1.46 ± 0.43
Depressive symptoms		
Point prevalence (%)	12	15.10 ± 1.10
Female:male sex ratio	7	1.32 ± 0.20

Note: Data are adapted from Boyd and Weisman (2).

[a] N = number of studies.

[b] SEM = standard error of the mean.

have encouraged a revolution in experimental psychiatry in which the hypotheses have been tested in clinical research. Many of the earlier hypotheses have been found wanting or simplistic. Nevertheless, they have led to increased understanding of the diagnosis, biology, and treatment of mood disorders and to newer research that represents a third level of development. This level, the focus of the present summary, promises to have practical clinical benefits now and in the near future.

Diagnosis and Terminology

For the purpose of orientation, a few comments on psychiatric nosology and the nature of theorizing in biological psychiatry may be helpful. The diagnosis of the severe mood disorders is complicated by a number of sometimes confusing terms and associated concepts.

The first important step occurred a century ago when Kraepelin boldly lumped a bewildering series of syndromes into the two major categories: manic-depressive illness and dementia praecox (schizophrenia). The first syndrome included all of the severe mood disorders (mania and melancholia), with or without an intermittent pattern of excitement alternating with depression (4,11). The manic-depressive concept survives today as a synonym for bipolar illness or, less often, as a generic term for severe mood disorders.

Recent diagnostic schemes have led to several ways of subdividing depressions. Most systems recognize some illnesses that are relatively minor ("neurotic," "reactive") and others that are currently referred to in the 1980 *Diagnostic and Statistical Manual* (1) as major. The latter include severe depressions (with or without episodes of mania) marked by

TABLE 2

Medical Characteristics of Major Depression

- Loss of energy, interest, sex drive, self-confidence
- Loss of appetite and weight
- Diminished bowel function
- Sleep disturbance (typically with early morning awakening and early onset of dream-sleep; slow onset and disturbed midsleep are also common; an atypical pattern is hypersomnia and tiredness throughout the day)
- Altered circadian rhythms: activity and temperature curves and several endocrine and other metabolic rhythms are abnormal, typically with an earlier acrophase (time of peak response) in each 24-hour cycle
- Increased secretion of corticosteroids and blunted response to several hormones that stimulate the anterior pituitary, such as thyrotropin-releasing hormone (TRH)
- Rhythmic changes in level of activity, anergy, mood, typically worse in morning
- Aches and pains (often including feelings of "pressure" in the head or chest)
- Feelings of anxiety and tension, sometimes with signs of autonomic overactivity (pulse, blood pressure, sweating)
- Loss of concentration; mild signs and symptoms of "pseudodementia" with some recent memory loss and confusion, especially in the elderly
- Change in posture, activity of facial muscles of expression
- Diminished self-care, poor performance at work and in social relations
- Obsessive rumination and preoccupations, sometimes including false interpretations of events or delusions concerning health, bodily function, intentions of others; impaired judgment
- Bipolar patients may present mixed picture of depression with psychotic excitement or appear more classically hypomanic or

10

TABLE 2 (continued)

manic, or they may present recurrent psychosis without hyperactivity of mania (especially when the syndrome is modified by medication, such as lithium salts); severe mania (Bell's syndrome) can include potentially fatal excitement to exhaustion following severe fluid and electrolyte disturbances secondary to mania
• High risk of self-injury, overdose, suicide

striking biologic signs and symptoms (such as loss of energy, libido, sleep, appetite, and intestinal function—all, typically, with some degree of daily or circadian rhythmicity), a tendency to remit and reoccur spontaneously, and apparent relative autonomy from life events or stresses (Table 2). Often (but not always) other psychiatric or medical illnesses are not present, and there is a relatively high incidence of similar disorders among close family members. These characteristics have supported the use of such terms as "endogenous," "endogenomorphic," "vital," "psychotic," or "melancholic" depressions. Patients with this subgroup of severe idiopathic illnesses are also most likely to respond favorably to modern medical treatments.

The apparently biological or endogenous forms of major medical depression are much more severe and persistent than common grief or human reactions to loss, stress, or disappointment. They are also to be differentiated clinically from patterns of illness and demoralization that are commonly encountered in connection with serious medical disorders, especially chronic infections, tumors, hepatic or renal failure, brain syndromes, intoxications, and metabolic or endocrine disorders (especially of the thyroid, parathyroid, and adrenal glands). A further differentiation has arisen from a research need to define relatively homogeneous groups of depressed patients who have "primary" depressions, that is, mood disorders that occur without additional complicating medical or other psychiatric disorders (4). Clinically, the value of this category (except as a reminder to apply a medical differential diagnostic approach) is somewhat limited, since some patients who have "secondary" depression have striking endogenomorphic or vital characteristics and respond well to antidepressants.

Yet another diagnostic dimension that is useful clinically and in research derives from the concept of "bipolar" versus "monopolar" mood disorders introduced by Leonhard (12) as a way of subdividing mood disorders into those with or without a strong individual and family history of psychotic or manic episodes. For etymologic consistency, "monopolar" has been changed to "unipolar" in the United States. The bipolar/unipolar (BP/UP) dichotomy is now considered to represent recurrent alternations of mood from normal euthymia into depression or into excited, manic, dysphoric, or psychotic states versus recurrent depression alone.

Other syndromes, including conditions marked by a mixture of disordered thinking (psychosis) and depression or excitement, have been called "schizoaffective" disorders. Still other disorders, marked by recurrent or episodic psychoses and substantial or full recovery between attacks, are sometimes referred to as "cycloid" psychoses in Europe, although the concept is not widely recognized in the United States. The status of these last two conditions as separate and distinct entities is uncertain. Indeed, there is strong support for the view that "schizoaffective" disorders cannot be distinguished meaningfully from bipolar manic-depressive illness by life history, family history, clinical and biological features in an acute exacerbation, response to lithium, or prognosis (13, 14).

Another condition that may be a variant of bipolar manic-depressive illness is the pattern of recurrent clinically significant depression with mild, spontaneous, and subclinical euphoria or hyperactivity and mild insomnia; this condition is sometimes referred to as "bipolar type II" disorder (15). Although there had been some concern as to the security of a distinction between unipolar and bipolar conditions based on a limited clinical exposure to patients with these conditions, good evidence now exists that mania and hypomania (mild mania) occur early in bipolar manic-depressive illnesses and that the rate of diagnostic error (*later* emergence of a bipolar pattern) is probably not more than about 5% (16).

Yet another matter of some uncertainty was whether the appearance of mania in a patient who had formerly only become depressed might be an artifact of treatment with an antidepressant agent or electroshock. Further, do such reactions (also known as the "switch process," whether spontaneous or associated with treatment) represent a separate diagnostic category from spontaneous manic-depressive mood swings or are they a matter of increased risk in certain vulnerable individuals (17)? Although the matter is not settled, recent research data indicate that the rate of appearance of mania spontaneously or following antidepressant treatments may be about the same (18); these rates vary widely among reported series, however—from less than 10% to more than 30% of episodes of illness (17, 18).

A further impression that has growing but still tentative support is that some cases of recurrent depression (apparently unipolar illnesses) may share biologic characteristics with more classic bipolar illnesses, including relatively early onset, a relatively strong family history of a mood disorder or related condition (such as alcoholism or acute psychoses), a relatively high attack frequency, and possibly long-term beneficial responses to a lithium salt (14,19,20).

In general, a keen clinical interest in mood disorders, or possible variants of mood disorders, is now evident, especially since the prognosis of these disorders tends to be relatively favorable, at least in their short-term responses to medical treatment (13,14). For example, it has recently been suggested that some acute paranoid illnesses of adult life may be forms of depression and may respond to treatment with an antidepressant drug rather than an antipsychotic agent (21). In addition, some conditions that develop commonly in certain medical or neurological disorders, such as stroke, may also be modifiable by treatment and not inevitable consequences of severe illness (22).

The tradition Kraepelin started a century ago—lumping severe mental illnesses into either manic-depressive or schizophrenic (dementia praecox) categories—thus continues. At present the tendency to see an increasing number of syndromes as mood disorders is on the ascent. Indeed, the concept of schizophrenia is in danger of extinction (23), since it is difficult to define, tends to have a low prevalence of similar conditions in close relatives, runs an unpredictable course (usually chronic), may or may not respond well to treatment, and lacks a consistent body of biologic characteristics.

This currently popular tendency to see an increasing number of conditions as mood disorders, or closely allied states, may be overdone. It is almost certain, for example, that the category of unipolar (perhaps better termed "nonbipolar") depression is heterogeneous biologically, in contrast to bipolar illnesses, which are coming close to the status of a discrete disease. Because the management and biomedical study of unipolar and bipolar illnesses have many close parallels, and because this general distinction appears to be useful, it will be retained in the discussion here.

An important source of general support for the diagnostic validity of these major categories of severe mood disorders, as well as a cornerstone of the credibility of a search for a biological basis of major depression and of manic-depressive illness, has been family and genetic studies, which will be considered next.

First, however, it may help orientation to reiterate that a major thrust of psychiatric research in the severe mood disorders over the past 30 years has been to define, for patients who have major mood disorders, biological characteristics that are diagnostically useful, that can help to optimize treatment, and that might point the way toward the pathophysiology or even to the causes of these idiopathic conditions. While there has been considerable progress toward a biologically and clinically sound diagnostic scheme and toward understanding some characteristics that can help to guide treatment, the search for primary causes so far has been unsuccessful. Indeed, virtually all of the biological characteristics of depressed or manic patients that have been defined are "state dependent" (that is, they disappear with recovery) and not stable biological traits or markers of a possibly heritable defect (24). Thus, while such state-dependent biological alterations can be useful for diagnosis and for guiding therapy, from a theoretical perspective they may merely be concomitant variations or secondary changes within the syndromes of depression and manic-depressive illness.

GENETICS

Family and genetic studies support both the search for biological explanations of major mood disorders and the search for improved biomedical diagnostic and therapeutic evaluations of patients who have major mood disorders. This approach indicates a strong genetic contribution in recurrent major depression and manic-depressive illness generally and provides especially strong support for the bipolar-unipolar distinction (24–36). Thus, as a general rule, family histories of severe mood disorders (manic or depressive) tend to be stronger among first-degree relatives of bipolar patients. Some recent family studies indicate that rates of mood disorders among first-degree relatives of patients who have bipolar depression are about twice those of the relatives of unipolar depressives (see Table 3) (29,36).

These morbid risk rates for unipolar depression are, in turn, at least two or three times above those believed to represent the risk in the general population, in which clinically significant mood disorders are reported to occur at prevalence rates of about 3–5% for men and perhaps 6–8% for women (5,36). Published prevalence rates of mood disorders have varied widely, however, with diagnostic criteria and methods of ascertainment (3); the rates currently average 5.3% for unipolar illness and less than 0.5% for bipolar illness (lifetime risk rates average 12% and 0.6%, respectively) (2). Studies have indicated that risk rates exceed 25% if a sibling and one parent are affected and exceed 40% if a sibling and both parents have a primary mood disorder (32); rates among close relatives tend to rise when the proband or index case had unipolar depression at a relatively early age of onset (below 40 years), and especially high morbid risk rates were found among same-sex relatives of bipolar or unipolar patients (30,36). In unipolar depression, female probands with an early onset tended to have a greater than normal number of female relatives with depressions, while male probands tended to have a greater than normal number not only of relatives with mood disorders but also of male relatives with sociopathic traits or alcoholism (30). These various details can be diagnostically helpful in evaluating cases of mood disorder.

TABLE 3
Family History in Bipolar (BP) or Unipolar (UP) Depression

Illness in First-Degree Relatives	Reference	Rates in Relatives (%)		
		Diagnoses in Index Case		
		BP	UP	Ratio
Mood disorder	29,36	19.0	13.0	1.5
Mania or affective psychosis	12,27,36	9.3	2.7	3.4
Bipolar	24	6.8	0.4	17.0
Unipolar	24	8.3	6.0	1.4

Note: Data are pooled from the reports and reviews cited above. In comparison, a control population had only a 5.5% rate of mood disorders among first-degree relatives, versus 10% for relatives of index cases with affective disorders (36). Since the rates of mood disorders vary markedly among studies, comparisons above are best made between columns, as is indicated by the BP:UP ratios. Note also that about half (40–70%) of mood disorders among relatives of BP index patients are depression only (35). In more recent studies based on direct interviews of relatives of index patients who had major mood disorders, the rates of illness have been lower than were typically reported in studies based on verbal reports or case records, and the rates among first-degree relatives of BP and UP index patients have been more similar, especially rates of unipolar depression in the family members (37).

It is important to point out that the most recent American studies, especially those based on direct examination or interviews of family members rather than on casual reports or case records only, have tended to find lower rates of indubitable mood disorders in first-degree relatives of both unipolar and bipolar index patients and a much smaller difference in family prevalence rates in relatives of bipolar than in those of unipolar patients than was formerly reported (37,38). For example, morbid risk rates among first-degree relatives of unipolar patients averaged 12%, and those for bipolar index patients were only slightly higher (at 14%) in a recent report, while the rate of mood disorders in a control population was 8% (37), a rate close to the average found in the general population (2). Again, unipolar illness was more common than bipolar illness or mania, even among relatives of bipolar index patients (in a ratio of about 2:1) (37).

These newer data add to the suggestion already proposed that unipolar and bipolar illnesses may have more in common than was formerly believed or, at least, that some forms of unipolar illness (possibly of early onset, great severity, and high rates of recurrence) may run in families that also have more typical bipolar illnesses. An alternative hypothesis might be that "severity" of mood disorder itself may be heritable. In general, a good deal of caution is warranted in interpreting the new and the older data, since the rates among studies have varied widely, as have the methods of case ascertainment.

Another interesting new idea is arising from a long-term epidemiologic study among the Amish of central Pennsylvania. Although there has been a consistent tendency for rates of depression (particularly in unipolar illnesses) to be much higher among females than males in the general population, this tendency did *not* obtain among the Amish, who have a

18

culture that strongly discourages alcoholism and antisocial behavior, which may be alternative behavior patterns for males in the general population in most cultures (39).

The Polarity Hypothesis

The early work of Leonhard that led to the current bipolar-unipolar concept was based mainly on the observation of a greater than normal occurrence of psychosis in the family backgrounds of patients with bipolar depression (12). There are now several additional studies (27,36,40) supporting the conclusion that rates of affective psychosis are three times as high among first-degree relatives of bipolar patients as among those of unipolar patients (see Table 3), especially in cases with an early age of onset of a bipolar disorder (Table 4) (40). Leonhard also suggested that there may be familial differences in personality types, so that close relatives of bipolar patients seem to include a greater than normal number with excited or hypomanic traits, while relatives of unipolar patients may have more depressive traits (12). A recent review of psychosocial factors in affective disorders suggested that "obsessive" traits were somewhat more characteristic of bipolar patients, while "neurotic" characteristics were common among unipolar patients (41). Similarly, bipolar patients tended to be married (often with a great deal of marital discord) and to have higher socioeconomic status than nonbipolar patients (41).

Not only do psychoses appear more frequently among close relatives of patients with bipolar manic-depressive illness, but severe psychiatric syndromes tend to "run true" in families. Thus, while the morbid risk of severe mood disorders (in a series of hundreds of patients and family members evaluated "blindly" by Winokur and his colleagues) among relatives of patients with affective disorders (unipolar or bipolar) was 10%, such illnesses appeared among only 3% of relatives of schizophrenic index patients—a rate that is similar to the value of 5.5% for relatives of normal subjects (36). Another clinically important point derived from follow-up studies is that the bipolar-unipolar distinction remains clini-

TABLE 4

Characteristics of Patients with Bipolar Manic-Depressive Illness vs. Age of Onset

Characteristic	Onset Age	
	≤29 (N = 78)	≥30 (N = 54)
First-degree relatives' morbid risk (%)		
All major mood disorders	14.2[a]	4.7
Bipolar illness	9.6[a]	0.8
Major depression	4.6	3.0
Alcoholism	17.2[a]	11.9
Sociopathy	1.5	1.9
Index age (years)	33.7	48.8[a]
Illness duration (years)	11.3	10.0
Episodes/year	2.3	2.4
Hospitalizations	5.0	4.7
Sex ratio (F/M)	1.9	3.5
Index admission severity score		
(% of max. possible)	82.5	80.0
Index improvement (%)	84.6	83.7
Index admission (days)	41.5	41.2
Neurological/Medical/EEG[b] history		
or symptoms or signs (%)	83.8	68.5

Note: Data adapted from Taylor and Abrams (40).

[a] Statistically significant by χ^2 (p<0.05 or less).

[b] Electroencephalographic.

cally sound over time, as was mentioned above. Rates of altered diagnosis were only about 5% overall in one report (16); 3–5%, depending on whether comparisons were made after only a month of follow-up, between a first and a second episode of illness, or after more than 10 years of follow-up in another study (36); and about 10% in a later study by the same investigators involving up to 40 years of follow-up (37).

There are also compelling data (although this is not a genetic point) that describe the natural history of recurrent manic-depressive illnesses from long-term follow-up studies (42,43). For either bipolar or unipolar illnesses, the mean cycle length *decreases* approximately logarithmically, from about three years from the initial episode to about a year after the fourth or fifth, and to less than a year after the sixth or seventh. Put in other terms, the risk of recurrence within two years is about 50% in a 50- to 60-year-old unipolar patient or a 40- to 50-year-old bipolar patient, but only about 20–30% for those in their twenties. That is, the risk of relapse in bipolar or unipolar recurrent affective disorders tends to *increase* with age.

Twin and Adoption Studies

A second important class of genetic data is derived from twin studies. Table 5 summarizes data from nine modern studies reviewed by several authors (26,28,33,36). These studies indicate much higher concordance rates between identical, or monozygotic (MZ), twins than between fraternal, or dizygotic (DZ), twins. In addition, the MZ:DZ ratio tends to be higher for bipolar illness than for unipolar ill ness. These data not only provide additional support for inherited contributions to risk for both bipolar and unipolar illness, but also suggest that this contribution may be stronger in bipolar manic-depressive illness (or that unipolar depression is a more heterogeneous cluster of syndromes).

A third important approach that is aimed at separating the contributions of environmental factors, learning, or experience (the "nature versus nurture" issue) is the study of adopted offspring. One of the few available studies of this type in severe mood disorders is that of Mendelwicz and Rainer (44). They found a greater frequency of mood disorders among the *biological* parents of the adopted proband cases (31% prevalence) than among the adopting parents (12%). In contrast, adopting and biological parents of control adoptees who did not have manic or depressive illnesses or who had a chronic neurological disorder had similar, low prevalence rates for mood disorders (6–10%), close to those

TABLE 5

Concordance Rates in Twins with Major Affective Disorders

| Category | Concordance Rates by Index Diagnosis (%) | |
	BP	UP
DZ	14	11
MZ	72	40
MZ:DZ ratio	5.1	3.6

Note: Data are pooled from reviews of nine published reports (26,28,33,36). Overall concordance rates for manic or depressive illness, regardless of polarity, are 68% and 19% for monozygotic (MZ) and dizygotic (DZ) twin pairs, respectively (MZ:DZ ratio = 3.6) (36). The groups above include more than 100 twin pairs. Among the rare instances (12 pairs) of MZ twins reared separately, the concordance rate for manic-depressive illness was 75% (25).

expected in the general population, while the parents of nonadopted manic or depressive patients had the expected high rate of such disorders (26%). When all psychiatric diagnoses were included, the rates were 40% versus 16% for biological versus adopting parents of index patients with mood disorders.

Another study (45) found a 38% prevalence of primary depressions among a small number of adoptees at least one of whose biological parents had such a disorder, compared with only 7% among a larger number of adoptees without such a parental history of mood disorder. Still other preliminary data from a study of Danish adoptees (46) indicates that suicide is 6.5 times more likely among biological than among adoptive relatives of 70 depressed adoptees. Again, strong support is provided by these several approaches for a familial, and probably an inherited, contribution to the risk of a major mood disorder.

AMINE HYPOTHESES

The next question that arises concerns the nature of the genetic contribution to the risk of depression or mania. In short, this is not known, although the genetic data just reviewed encourage the search for biological as well as putative developmental or psychosocial factors in major mood disorders. The most prominent of the hypotheses that have been considered over the past two decades have implicated altered function of one or more monoamines acting as synaptic neurotransmitters or modulatory neurohormones at nerve terminals in the central nervous system (CNS).

Among the earliest formulations of such amine-based hypotheses concerning the biology of mood disorders were those made by Everett and Tolman (47) and by Jacobsen (48) in 1959, although clinical studies of amine metabolism in patients with mood disorders had been carried out by Weil-Malherbe (49) even earlier in that decade. The most-often-mentioned amines have been the catecholamine norepinephrine (NE) (50) and the indoleamine serotonin—5-hydroxytryptamine (5-HT) (51). In addition, there have been considerations of altered function of acetylcholine (ACh) (52) as well as of the catecholamine dopamine (DA) (53), a transmitter in its own right as well as the immediate precursor of norepinephrine.

All of these substances are known to be synthesized, stored in, and released from specific neuronal fibers in the brain, spinal cord, or peripheral nervous system. These systems have been well characterized and their detailed biology is reviewed elsewhere (54–58). In addition, several diagrams are included here to summarize the salient features of the anatomical distribution of monoaminergic systems in the mammalian brain, as well as the biochemical and metabolic functional organization of amine-producing nerve terminals. These figures show that catecholamines (norepinephrine and dopamine) arise in bilaterally symmetrical groups of neuronal cell bodies in the midbrain and brainstem, respectively (Figure 1). These cells project widely.

The noradrenergic neurons project mainly through dorsal and ventral fiber bundles that concentrate in the median forebrain bundle—the major conduit through which many aminergic fibers course to the diencephalon and forebrain. This structure is a site at which electrodes placed in the brain of a laboratory animal elicit extraordinarily high rates of self-stimulation, implicating these tracts in arousal and behav-

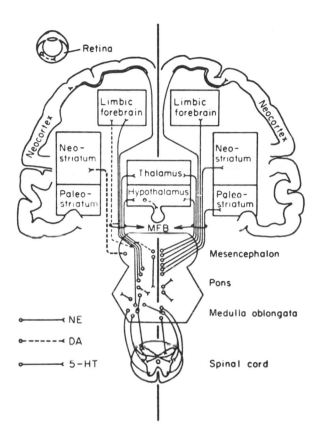

Labels in figure:
Retina
Limbic forebrain | Limbic forebrain
Neocortex | Neocortex
Neo-striatum | Neo-striatum
Paleo-striatum | Paleo-striatum
Thalamus
Hypothalamus
MFB
Mesencephalon
Pons
Medulla oblongata
Spinal cord

NE
DA
5-HT

FIGURE 1

**Schematic Organization of Monoamine-Containing Neurons of
the Mammalian Central Nervous System**

Note: The diagram is organized with the catecholamine systems on the left and the
serotonin systems on the right. The catecholamines are norepinephrine (NE) and
dopamine (DA); the indoleamine serotonin is 5-hydroxytryptamine (5-HT). Cell

ioral reinforcement mechanisms. A mere few thousand noradrenergic cells account for virtually all of the projections throughout the CNS of norepinephrine-containing neuron fibers, including the spinal cord, where relationships with the central neurons of the sympathetic nervous system occur. The same cells are known to project to such widely separate regions as the cerebellum and cerebral cortex.

Dopamine occurs not only as the immediate precursor of norepinephrine in noradrenergic neurons of the CNS and the peripheral sympathetic nervous system, but also as a neurotransmitter in its own right that has major projections to the basal ganglia, the limbic system, and portions of the frontal and temporal lobes, as well as small projections in the retina and within the hypothalamus. The dopamine systems in the forebrain are believed to be a major site of action of antipsychotic agents that are effective in mania and are used adjunctively with antidepressants in the management of psychotic forms of depression. The extrapyramidal actions of these drugs are probably accounted for by their antidopamine effects in the basal ganglia, and their antipsychotic and antimanic effects may be related to antagonism of this neurotransmitter in the limbic or cortical regions. Their ability

---

bodies of norepinephrine neurons are few in number and are highly localized in the locus ceruleus and nearby cells of the pons and medulla; they project to the spinal cord and to the diencephalon and forebrain rather diffusely. Dopamine projections are more selective to the basal ganglia (nigrostriatal pathway), as well as from midbrain to limbic structures and to frontal and temporal cerebral cortex (mesolimbic and mesocortical projections). Dopamine cells also occur in the retina and hypothalamus. Serotonin projections are even more widespread than those of norepinephrine and arise from a series of nuclei in pons and brainstem (raphe nuclei). This scheme is based on the work of Andén and co-workers (54) as is reviewed elsewhere (55–58).

to elevate prolactin and alter other functions of the hypothalamus and pituitary is accounted for by their interactions with hypothalamic dopamine systems, notably the tuberinfundibular system, which releases dopamine as a neurohormone into the hypophysioportal blood vessels to reach the anterior pituitary.

Projections of serotonin-containing neurons are similar to those of norepinephrine cells, except that the cell bodies are localized along the midline in the raphe nuclei of the midbrain and brainstem. These projections are believed to influence sleep, hypothalamic functions, and affective arousal, as well as motor function. It has recently been suggested that such indoleamine-producing cells may also produce other highly active substances that may act as neurohormones. This suggestion is now quite clearly established for some serotonin cells, which also produce the peptide substance P. A similar process appears to be true of dopamine cells, some of which may also produce cholecystokinin, another peptide hormone formerly believed to occur only in the gut.

Figure 2 summarizes the metabolic organization of catecholamine-producing neurons. In the process of producing catecholamines, the rate-limiting and physiologically critical step is the hydroxylation of tyrosine to form dihydroxyphenylalanine (DOPA). The next step of decarboxylation of this amino acid to dopamine is relatively easy, due to the abundance and lack of saturation of the aromatic amino acid decarboxylases by their substrate amino acids under physiologic conditions. In some cells, an additional enzyme, dopamine-β-hydroxylase (DBH), also occurs to permit the conversion of dopamine to norepinephrine. Dopaminergic neurons lack this enzyme, however, whereas dopamine acts as a neurotransmitter in its own right. Additional systems are

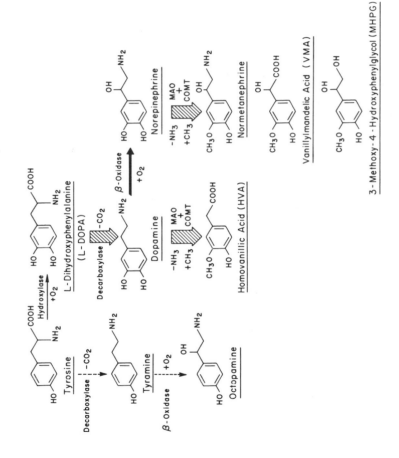

FIGURE 2

Catecholamine Metabolic Pathway

Note: Catecholamines and other related phenethylamines are produced from phenylalanine and tyrosine. The size of the arrows suggests the relative magnitude of activity through each enzymatic step. The hydroxylation of tyrosine is rate-limiting because of the small amount of hydroxylase only in catecholamine cells and its near-saturation with substrate under normal conditions. Decarboxylation occurs through a widely distributed aromatic amino acid decarboxylase enzyme, which is probably very similar, if not identical, for virtually all aromatic amines. In norepinephrine cells only, dopamine can be further oxidized at the 2 (β) position of the side-chain by dopamine-β-oxidase, or dopamine-β-hydroxylase (DBH), to yield norepinephrine. Metabolic inactivation occurs through the actions of monoamine oxidase (MAO) and catechol-O-methyl transferase (COMT), which uses S-adenosylmethionine (a putative antidepressant) as cofactor. The deaminated and O-methylated products include normetanephrine, vanillylmandelic acid (VMA), and 3-methoxy-4-hydroxyphenethyleneglycol (MHPG) from norepinephrine, as well as 3-methoxytyramine, 3,4-dihydroxyphenylacetic acid (DO-PAC), and homovanillic acid (HVA) from dopamine. In addition, some cells also produce epinephrine (N-methylated norepinephrine), as well as other trace amines including tyramine and octopamine, which may arise separately in other cells, or with catecholamines, and be released with them as cotransmitters; certain peptides may also be produced in catecholamine cells, including cholecystokinin in dopamine cells, as additional cotransmitters or neurohormones. While it was formerly believed that MHPG might be a uniquely representative CNS metabolite of norepinephrine, it is now clear that much urinary MHPG arises from peripheral metabolism and that much of the MHPG that comes from brain is converted in the periphery to VMA to contribute to its appearance in the urine.

known to occur in lower organisms to convert tyrosine directly to the amines tyramine and octopamine. Although these are present, they are less prominent in mammalian brain, and their physiologic or potential pathophysiologic significance is not clear.

The metabolic inactivation of the catecholamines is similar for both dopamine and norepinephrine, which are both acted on by the enzymes monoamine oxidase (MAO) and catechol-O-methyl transferase (COMT) to yield a variety of metabolites that are either deaminated or O-methylated, or both. These inactive metabolites include, notably, methoxytyramine, dihydroxyphenylacetic acid (DOPAC), and homovanillic acid (HVA) from dopamine (respectively methylated, deaminated, and both) and, analogously, normetanephrine, 3-methoxy-4-hydroxyphenethyleneglycol (MHPG), and vanillylmandelic acid (VMA) from norepinephrine. Tyramine and octopamine also are acted on by MAO. While these metabolic forms of inactivation are important, it is almost certain that the most critical means of inactivation of the catecholamines (and serotonin) at the synapse is a process of active reuptake back into the presynaptic neuron. This step is an important site of action of stimulants such as amphetamines and cocaine, as well as of imipramine-like antidepressant agents, as will be further discussed later.

The availability of the deaminated or O-methylated metabolites of the catecholamines has made it possible to assay their levels in urine, plasma, or cerebrospinal fluid (CSF) in humans, including depressed patients. The acidic metabolites, such as HVA and VMA, as well as 5-hydroxyindoleacetic acid (5-HIAA) produced from the catecholamines or serotonin, respectively, are removed into the venous blood at the choroid plexus by a process of active transport that is selectively blocked by probenecid. Thus, it has been possible to measure the rate of rise of acidic metabolites of amines in the CSF following a large dose of probenecid as an index of the rate of production and utilization of monoamines in the CNS. This technique has been applied repeatedly to the study of patients with depression, as will be discussed in the next section. The status of MHPG as a relatively unique metabolite of central norepinephrine metabolism is currently insecure, since it is known that large amounts of MHPG are produced by peripheral metabolism of norepinephrine as well as by metabolism in the brain and spinal cord; moreover, there is a brisk peripheral conversion of MHPG to VMA. In short, while levels of MHPG in plasma or its excretion in the urine may have some general relationship to the function of catecholamine neurons in the CNS and the sympathetic nervous system, this relationship is not unique to the brain.

Other aspects of the metabolic apparatus under discussion have also been evaluated extensively in depressed patients. These evaluations have included assays of amines and their metabolites in postmortem brain tissue of suicides, assays of CSF levels of metabolites with or without pretreatment with probenecid, measurements of plasma levels of norepinephrine or even of the enzyme DBH (both of which are believed to be released by activity in noradrenergic nerve terminals and to reflect the activity of such neurons), activity of MAO in blood platelets or other tissues (such as from skin or intestinal biopsies), and activity of COMT in erythrocytes. Additional measurements that can be applied to patients have included assessments of amine transport mechanisms (especially for serotonin) in blood platelets, ion transport in erythrocytes, and binding sites for putative receptors of amines or antidepressant drugs on leukocytes prepared from blood.

The metabolic arrangements for the production and inactivation of serotonin (5-HT) (summarized in Figure 3) are

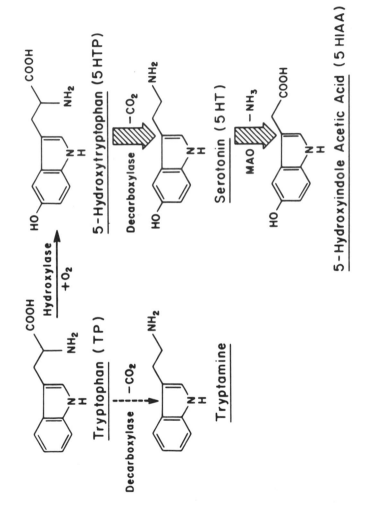

Tryptophan (TP)

Hydroxylase
+O₂

5-Hydroxytryptophan (5HTP)

Decarboxylase
−CO₂

Serotonin (5HT)

MAO
−NH₃

5-Hydroxyindole Acetic Acid (5HIAA)

Decarboxylase
−CO₂

Tryptamine

FIGURE 3

Serotonin Metabolic Pathway

Note: The arrangements at serotonin-producing nerve terminals are similar to those for catecholamine cells, as depicted in Figure 2. Thus, tryptophan, the precursor amino acid, is first ring-hydroxylated to 5-hydroxytryptophan (5-HTP), which is, in turn, decarboxylated to the amine serotonin, or 5-HT. The major route of metabolic inactivation of 5-HT is by mitochondrial MAO to yield the end-product 5-hydroxyindoleacetic acid (5-HIAA). This and other acid products of monoamine metabolism (such as HVA and VMA) are removed into the venous blood at the choroid plexus by a probenecid-sensitive transport process.

very similar to those for the catecholamines. In this case, the precursor amino acid is tryptophan, an essential metabolite whose absence in the diet can lead to pellagra (formerly considered a psychiatric illness). Since the 5-hydroxylating enzyme for this amino acid is not fully saturated with substrate in the intact brain, large doses of tryptophan, as well as of 5-hydroxytryptophan (5-HTP), can be given to increase production of serotonin (and of other indoleamines, such as tryptamine). In the catecholamine pathways, large doses of tyrosine are much less able to push the production of dopamine or norepinephrine, while large doses of L-DOPA can increase synthesis of dopamine (and, to a much lesser extent, of norepinephrine).

These facts are the basis for repeated attempts at the "metabolic" treatment of depression with large doses of DOPA on the one hand, or of tryptophan or 5-HTP on the other (either alone or with an inhibitor of MAO to increase amine levels even more). Despite the benefits of DOPA therapy in Parkinson's disease (a known state of deficiency of dopamine in the basal ganglia due to the idiopathic degeneration of nigrostriatal dopamine-producing neurons), this clever approach to the experimental therapeutics of depression and the testing of amine hypotheses of the pathophysiology of depression has had little success, as will be reviewed later.

Figures 4 and 5 indicate the organization of catecholamine and indoleamine nerve terminals, respectively. At catecholamine terminals, the amine product (dopamine or norepinephrine, and possibly additional cotransmitters, such as trace amines like octopamine, or peptides) is released by a depolarizing nerve impulse that requires calcium ions and that is believed to involve exocytosis or the fusion of the presynaptic vesicle membranes with the cell plasma membrane to provide exit for the vesicular contents. These contents may include vesicular enzymes as well as stored amine molecules, as has already been mentioned regarding the co-release of norepinephrine and of DBH. Levels of either of these in plasma may be clinically applicable indices of activity of noradrenergic nerve terminals (especially those of the peripheral sympathetic nervous system). The released amine exerts a selective effect at receptors located at nearby postsynaptic cell membranes.

There are believed to be specific receptors for dopamine as well as α and β receptors for norepinephrine (and for the small amounts of epinephrine also produced in the brainstem). These adrenergic receptors are similar to those related to the function of the peripheral sympathetic nervous system. As in the peripheral autonomic noradrenergic nervous system, there is also evidence of presumably presynaptic "autoreceptors" for dopamine and for norepinephrine; for the latter, these have pharmacologic characteristics of α_2 adrenergic receptors. In the cases of dopamine and norepinephrine, it is believed that the autoreceptors can throttle the synthesis and release of the respective catecholamine neurotransmitters.

The functions of postsynaptic α_1 and β receptors in the CNS are obscure; it is known, however, that β and dopamine receptors in the brain, like β receptors in peripheral tissues, are linked to and stimulate the activity of the enzyme adenylate cyclase in membranes, which converts adenosine-triphosphate (ATP) to $3',5'$-cyclic-adenosine-monophosphate (cyclic-AMP or cAMP). This last product (cyclic-AMP) is believed to act as a "second messenger" of many hormones as well as neurotransmitters to carry out their ef-

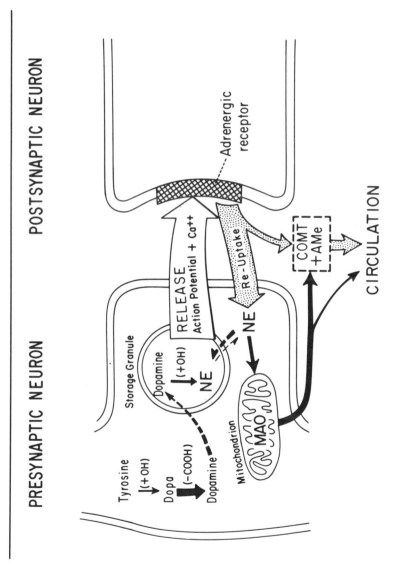

FIGURE 4

Organization of a Catecholamine Synapse

Note: The metabolic apparatus summarized in Figure 2 is located in specific portions of the presynaptic neuron. Amine transmitter is released by depolarizing nerve impulses in the presence of Ca^{++} by a process of exocytotic fusion of presynaptic vesicles and cell membrane to provide amine in the synaptic cleft. The transmitter is recognized by specific receptor sites on the postsynaptic cell surface. These include α_1 and β receptors in the case of norepinephrine (and presumably β receptors for the few epinephrine neurons that occur), and DA receptors at dopamine-releasing terminals. It is also believed that autoreceptors occur for dopamine (DA receptors) and norepinephrine (α_2 receptors) and that these help to control (throttle) the synthesis and release of catecholamine neurotransmitters. Inactivation occurs mainly by a reuptake process sensitive to stimulant and antidepressant agents. Also, some scavenging of leftover amine occurs through the actions of MAO and of COMT, with its cofactor S-adenosylmethionine (S-AMe), to yield the O-methylated and oxidatively deaminated metabolites outlined in Figure 2.

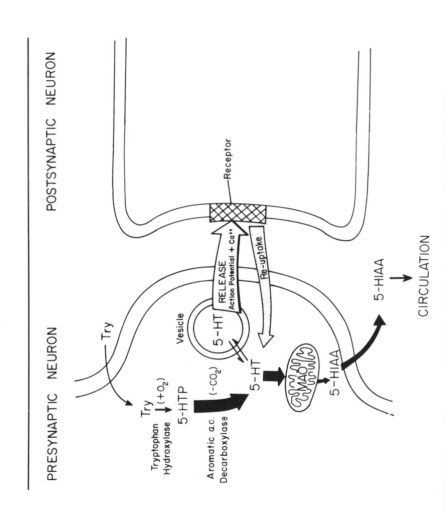

FIGURE 5

Organization of a Serotonin Synapse

Note: The principal features are similar to those of catecholamine synapses, shown in Figure 4. The presynaptic nerve terminals contain the metabolic system outlined in Figure 3. Release, reuptake, and inactivation by MAO are similar to those steps described for catecholamines in Figure 4. The arrangements of receptors and their precise characterization in the serotonin system are not as well developed as in the catecholamine systems. The precursor is L-tryptophan (Try), which is converted to 5-HTP and thence to 5-HT, which can be deaminated to 5-HIAA, as described in detail in Figure 3. In this and the preceding three figures, the sizes of the arrows suggest the relative activity or abundance of each enzymatic step. There is now evidence that the peptide substance P may be produced with serotonin in some cells and may be released as a cotransmitter or additional neurohormone. Substance P is a strongly neuropharmacologically active neuron-depolarizing substance, although there are as yet no drugs known to interact specifically with it or with other amine cotransmitter peptides.

fects in receptive cells. Its levels in plasma, as well as its stimulation in blood cells, have been evaluated in depressed patients.

Finally, the arrangements at a serotonin nerve terminal are depicted in Figure 5. The arrangements for the synthesis and storage of serotonin are very similar to those believed to exist for catecholamine at catecholamine nerve terminals. Release again requires depolarizing stimulation in the presence of calcium ions, and inactivation is accomplished partly by reuptake, as well as by the actions of MAO. In serotonin neurons, the role of MAO is probably more important physiologically than it is in catecholamine cells, since it is believed that there is a constant "spill-over" of newly synthesized indoleamine from storage vesicles to MAO.

Serotonin receptors are believed to exist at the postsynaptic cell surface, but these are not well characterized, nor are their physiologic actions clear. Also, few drugs are highly selective in blocking serotonin receptors, although several partly selective agents exist, including the hallucinogen lysergic acid diethylamide (LSD). In contrast, several agents, including some with antidepressant activity, selectively block the presynaptic reuptake of serotonin, as will be discussed later. The possibility of increasing the rate of production and spill-over of serotonin by giving large doses of the precursor amino acids tryptophan or 5-HTP has already been mentioned. It has also been pointed out that uptake of serotonin by blood platelets has been studied in depressed patients and that studies have been made of patients' urinary and CSF levels of 5-HIAA, the end-product of the metabolism of serotonin, as well.

The organization of nerve terminals for acetylcholine (ACh) is also similar to those shown for the other monoamines. The distribution of ACh pathways is less well understood, due to the lack of highly specific histological markers of these neurons. Some cholinergic systems are intrinsic to the neocortex and the basal ganglia, but others sweep into the forebrain from the brainstem. There is also an important cortical input from the limbic system that is believed to degenerate in Alzheimer's dementia. ACh is produced from the precursor choline by the actions of choline-acetyl transferase (CAT) and the cofactor acetyl-coenzyme-A (acetyl-CoA). ACh is not taken up, but choline is, and this process may help to regulate ACh synthesis. The product is rapidly inactivated by enzymatic hydrolysis by acetylcholinesterase (AChE). Most of the ACh receptors in the brain are believed to be muscarinic in type.

It should be apparent from the considerations just reviewed that monoaminergic neuronal systems are especially well suited, by their location and actions, for involvement in the major mood disorders, at least hypothetically. Thus, the CNS monoamine systems are widely and diffusely distributed and appear to subserve tonic background activities that occur over a long time base and that include regulation of autonomic functions, arousal, sleep, sex and aggression, movement, daily cycles, and hypothalamic-pituitary function.

The Pharmacologic Basis of Amine Hypotheses

Support for the amine hypotheses derives mainly from analysis of the differential actions of drugs on behavior in experimental animals and on mood in patients or other human subjects. This pharmacologic literature is large and complex (50,51,56,58,59); its essence is summarized in Table 6. The main theme that arises from these observations is that treatments that deplete, inhibit the synthesis of, or block the

41

TABLE 6

Effects of Drugs on the Metabolism of Amines in the CNS

Function of Drug	Drug	Action	Behavioral Effects
Precursor	L-DOPA	DA increased	Agitation
	Tryptophan	5-HT increased	Usually sedative, anti-manic(?)
	Choline or lecithin	ACh increased	Depressant(?), antimanic(?)
Inhibit synthesis	α-Me-p-tyrosine (AMPT)	Blocks tyrosine hydroxylase, lowers CA levels	Sedative, antihypertensive
	α-Me-DOPA (Aldomet)	Blocks decarboxylase	Sedative, antihypertensive, depressant
	Disulfiram, fusaric acid	Block β-hydroxylase, lower NE, raise DA	Little effect, some depression, some excitement on withdrawal
	p-Cl-phenylalanine (PCPA)	Blocks tryptophan hydroxylase, lowers 5-HT	Aggression, hypersexuality, insomnia

Decrease retention	α-Me-dopa[a]	False transmitter replaces endogenous CA	Sedative, antihypertensive, depressant
	Reserpine,[a] tetrabenazine	Block storage in vesicles, lower amine levels	Sedative, depressant, antihypertensive
Alter membrane crossing	Amphetamines	Increase release, decrease reuptake (some MAO inhibition)	Stimulant, anorexic, psychotogenic
	Cocaine	Decreases reuptake	Stimulant, euphoriant
	Heterocyclic antidepressants (HCAs)	Mainly block reuptake (weak MAO inhibition), increase sensitivity of 5-HT and α-NE receptors, decrease sensitivity of β-NE receptors	Antidepressant
	Lithium salts	Decrease release of NE and DA	Antimanic, mood-stabilizing
Block receptors	Neuroleptics	Mainly blockade of DA receptors	Antimanic, antipsychotic, sedative
	Methysergide	Mainly blockade of indoleamine receptors	Weakly antimanic(?)

TABLE 6

Effects of Drugs on the Metabolism of Amines in the CNS (continued)

Function of Drug	Drug	Action	Behavioral Effects
Block receptors	Atropine	Blocks muscarinic receptors	Intoxicant
Inhibit catabolism	MAO inhibitors	Block MAO, increase amine levels	Antidepressant, euphoriant
	Polyphenols (e.g., butylgallate)	Block COMT	Little effect or toxic
	Physostigmine	Block cholinesterase	Depressant(?), antimanic(?)

Note: DA = dopamine, NE = norepinephrine, CA = catecholamine, Me = methyl, COMT = catechol-O-methyl transferase.

[a] Depression associated with antihypertensive (anticatecholamine) agents is a problem in clinical practice. About 15% of patients given reserpine (especially those with a history of depression) reportedly become significantly depressed (timing is *unpredictable*; the cause-effect relationship is tenuous and probably requires a susceptible host).

actions of monoamines (notably, the catecholamines) tend to induce depression in susceptible subjects (60) or at least to induce sedation, behavioral underarousal, or antiautonomic effects; treatments that increase the availability or actions of the catecholamines have stimulating or arousing actions. The effects of increasing or decreasing the actions of serotonin or ACh tend to be opposite to those involving norepinephrine or dopamine. That is, enhancing the effects of serotonin or ACh tends to be similar to diminishing the effects of catecholamines.

This reciprocal tendency may seem confusing, since most of the available metabolic support for amine hypotheses in depression (although it suggests a deficiency of catecholamines or an excess of ACh function) also suggests a deficiency of serotonin in depression. Perhaps the most reasonable way in which to consider such ideas is to suspect that any single-amine hypothesis that would account for the entire complex of signs and symptoms in depression and mania is almost certainly oversimplified, while the altered function of individual amine systems might contribute to specific features of the syndrome. For example, it is not unreasonable to suppose that increased function of dopamine might lead to mania or psychosis (61), while a lack of dopamine might lead to anhedonia and psychomotor retardation; that a deficiency of norepinephrine might lead to anergy and anhedonia too, or that its excess might contribute to agitation or mania; that a lack of serotonin might also contribute to agitation and insomnia; that an excess of ACh might add to psychomotor retardation and depressed mood; or that dysfunction in any of these systems might contribute to altered biorhythms that are now increasingly documented in severe depression and mania.

It is important to realize that this way of developing biological hypotheses in psychiatric research has been dominant in the past 20 years. Despite the attractiveness and seeming rationality of this inductive approach, it suffers from potentially fallacious logic when applied to pathophysiology or etiology. Thus, a typical proposition is that, if antidepressant treatments tend to increase the function of norepinephrine or serotonin (62–70) (see Table 7 and the next chapter) and antimanic treatments tend to diminish the function of catecholamines (9), then their opposite might reflect the pathophysiology of the illness under treatment. While such notions might be heuristic or experimentally testable, they

TABLE 7

General Actions of Antidepressants and Antimanic Agents

Agent	Actions
Antidepressants	MAO inhibitors prevent inactivation of catecholamines and serotonin (5-HT)
	Imipramine and other HCAs prevent uptake of NE or 5-HT and may increase release or alter sensitivity of some receptors after repeated treatment
	ECT may mimic many effects of HCAs on amine metabolism, but action mechanisms remain obscure
Antimanic agents	Neuroleptic-antipsychotic agents block DA receptors
	Lithium salts block release of catecholamines (NE and DA) and may stabilize some receptors, as well as having still-obscure effects on cation distribution at neurons

may be no more logical than it would be to assume a state of penicillin deficiency in general paresis of the insane (even though the drug helps the illness) or a renal tubular defect in congestive heart failure (even though thiazide diuretics relieve edema). Moreover, they are based on a still very incomplete understanding of the actions of mood-altering agents.

One additional curious effect of the amine hypotheses has been their interaction with the process of developing potential new mood-altering agents. In general, there have been remarkably few fundamentally new medical treatments for depression or mania since the somewhat fortuitous clinical discovery of the antidepressant effects of MAO inhibitors and imipramine, or of the antimanic actions of lithium salts and chlorpromazine—all prior to 1960 (8).

A partial understanding of the actions of these agents focused attention on their interactions with the monoamines and may have contributed to screening tests that have led to ever-larger numbers of similar agents, as well as a possibly excessively narrow focus on such amines in the pathophysiology of affective disorders. Most of the newer antidepressants have been discovered by screening compounds for blocking actions against catecholamine uptake (e.g., amoxapine, trimipramine, maprotiline, mianserin, nomifensin, viloxazine, and metabolites of clomipramine), serotonin uptake (e.g., clomipramine, femoxetine, and zimelidine), or anti-MAO activity (e.g., chlorgyline) (71,72). Iprindole may be a notable exception, although its efficacy in severe endogenous depressions is not well established (72).

The attempt to test the amine hypotheses of mood disorders in clinical experiments has led to much work using several clever clinical research strategies that are summa-

47

rized in Table 8. Most of this work has involved tests of a catecholamine or indoleamine hypothesis (49–52,56,60,73–77).

Comments on Amine Hypotheses

Overall, the clinical research evidence favoring hypotheses on amine deficiency or excess in depression or mania is weak. The effects of experimental pharmacologic interventions—as shown in Table 6, excluding accepted standard treatments with heterocyclic antidepressants (HCAs), MAO inhibitors, lithium salts, and neuroleptics—do not provide compelling support. For example, loading patients with amino acids that are precursors (Figures 2–5) of amines

---

TABLE 8

Clinical Strategies to Test Amine Hypotheses in Mood Disorders

- Interpretation of differential drug responses (improvement vs. worsening)
- Precursor loading (tryptophan, 5-HTP, DOPA)
- Metabolite excretion vs. clinical state or treatment (especially urinary 5-HIAA or MHPG)
- CSF metabolites (basal or after probenecid to block removal) vs. diagnosis or clinical state (5-HIAA, MHPG, VMA, or HVA)
- Neuroendocrine responses that may be secondary to altered amine function (cortisol, growth hormone, prolactin)
- Postmortem levels of brain metabolites (DA, NE, 5-HT, MHPG, HVA, 5-HIAA), especially in suicides
- Enzyme, transport, or receptor activities (brain, plasma, platelets, red blood cells) (tyrosine hydroxylase, DBH, MAO, COMT, serotonin uptake, α- or β-adrenergic receptors)

(73,78,79) or running trials of inhibitors of amine synthesis (77,80) are both known to alter amine turnover in the human CNS, based on studies of metabolites in CSF (80). Yet these approaches have not provided a useful antidepressant or antimanic treatment to date.

Stimulants such as amphetamines provide an interesting model of manic-depressive illness, since intoxication in stimulant abusers results in lithium-sensitive (81) euphoria, followed by agitation and paranoid psychosis (as in mania), followed by depression ("crashing") (76,82–84). Nevertheless, their effects in clinical depression are at best transitory in most cases, and they worsen agitation in many cases (85,86). In mania, stimulants or other dopamine agonists can even induce a paradoxical beneficial effect, although this may reflect selective stimulation of autoreceptors to *diminish* CA availability (87–89).

Interesting preliminary suggestions of benefits have recently been obtained with the serotonin agonist fenfluramine in mania and depression (75), with the DA agonist piribedil in depression (80), and with the α-NE agonist clonidine (90), the anticholinesterase physostigmine (91), and the ACh precursor choline (or lecithin) in mania (92,93). These observations have arisen directly from attempts to test amine hypotheses. It is also important to realize that certain antihypertensive (antisympathetic, or antinoradrenergic) agents such as reserpine and α-methyldopa (Aldomet) are associated with clinically significant depression (see Table 6) (60,77).

In metabolic tests of amine hypotheses, the catecholamines (Table 9) and serotonin (Table 10) are by far the most extensively evaluated. Data for Tables 9 and 10 were obtained from previous reviews concerning catecholamines (50,76), 5-HT (51,75,94), or both (53,56,74,77,79); the tables

TABLE 9

Clinical Evidence Concerning a Catecholamine Hypothesis in Major Mood Disorders

Measure	Available Studies (N)	Proportion Supportive (%)	Comments
Postmortem regional brain chemistry			
NE	3	33	Regions inconsistent; one study found HVA higher
DA	3	33	
HVA	1	0	
Urinary MHPG			
All depressed	11	82	Most studies are from three labs and have small numbers and much overlap in small decreases among diagnostic groups and controls
BP vs. UP	3	100	All three found BP patients 30% lower; two also found depressed schizoaffective (BP?) lower than UP (36%), but these differences are similar to interlab differences in same diagnostic groups

To predict response to HCAs	9	67	Most studies dealt with few variables and small numbers; two other studies unable to draw conclusions due to high response rates or high MHPG variance
CSF metabolites (depression)			
MHPG	5	40	Poor correlation with urinary MHPG; cannot use probenecid for MHPG; MHPG probably unchanged in mania but not adequately studied
HVA	1	0	
VMA			UP patients tend to have lower VMA; with probenecid, not all are significantly lower; suggest subgroups
Basal	12	67	
Probenecid	9	67	
CSF metabolites (mania)			
Basal	6	0	All studies found low or normal VMA; one found increased rise of VMA
Probenecid	3	33	
Enzyme activities			
Platelet MAO	7	14	Four studies suggest *low* MAO; in BP patients, two found lower, one higher than UP patients
Red blood cell COMT	5	20	Two studies found *low* COMT; another suggested better response to HCAs with lower COMT
Plasma DBH	6	20	One study found low DBH (in UP cases)

TABLE 10

Clinical Evidence Concerning a Serotonin Hypothesis in Major Mood Disorders

Measure	Available Studies (N)	Proportion Supportive (%)	Comments
Postmortem regional brain chemistry			
5-HT	7	57	Only 10% mean decrease in most studies
5-HIAA	5	40	Only 15% mean decrease, but very inconsistent among CNS regions
5-HT or Try in plasma or CSF	5	20	Small changes, highly inconsistent
CSF 5-HIAA in depressions			
Basal	15	47	Up to 70% decrease in four studies; trend to decrease in 12, but increases in two studies; subgroup suggested
Probenecid	9	67	Up to 60% less accumulation
CSF 5-HIAA in mania			
Basal	6	50	All studies find 5-HIAA normal or low; none elevated
Probenecid	3	67	

CSF 5-HIAA to differentiate UP and BP			
Basal	3	67	Decreased in UP only
Probenecid	3	33	Decreased in BP only; these results contradictory, although three out of six do suggest about 30% decrease in UP + BP series
Effect of HCAs on CSF 5-HIAA	8	100	All find decreases of 10–49% in basal and 31% less rise after probenecid
Try or 5-HTP as antidepressant	10	40	Only one double-blind positive study but 40% suggest some possible benefits alone or with HCAs, MAO inhibitors, or ECT; CSF 5-HIAA does rise
PCPA as antimanic (blocks 5-HT synthesis)	1	0	Not effective in mania; effects in depression poorly evaluated

provide illustrative summaries but are not exhaustive reviews. As these tables illustrate, the data supporting a deficiency of catecholamines or serotonin in depression and the opposite in mania are, frankly, meager and inconsistent.

One of the few repeatedly observed relationships is a fall in urinary MHPG with depression (95) and its return to normal values with recovery (76) or switch (17) into mania. There are also suggestions that low levels of MHPG excretion may be more characteristic (or more easily observed) in bipolar depression (76,95). There are several reports of attempts to predict responses to specific types of imipramine-like HCAs from initial values of urinary MHPG excretion. The idea has been that low levels of MHPG may predict responsiveness to drugs that have relatively strong effects on norepinephrine uptake into neurons (desipramine, maprotiline, or imipramine), whereas higher values may predict responsiveness to agents that are less selective and that also have strong effects against serotonin uptake (clomipramine or amitriptyline) (96). However, these ideas are based on the study, as of 1981, of a total of only 71 patients who had low levels of MHPG and 53 who had high levels of MHPG; at least four recent studies have failed to support the predictions (97) or produced equivocal results (98). Still other recent reports are somewhat more encouraging (95,99,100).

Nevertheless, the marked interindividual and interlaboratory variance in MHPG assays suggests that this approach may not lead readily to practical routine clinical methods (101). Indeed, the circadian variation in MHPG excretion is about 30–40% in normal subjects and manic-depressive patients, while the mean difference between controls and bipolar or unipolar depressed patients is only about 20–40% (102). Other recent findings that cast further doubt on the idea that urinary MHPG levels may selectively reflect metabolism of norepinephrine in the CNS are that much of MHPG is converted to VMA and that 20% or less of urinary MHPG may derive from central metabolism of norepinephrine (103).

Among studies of indoleamine metabolism, some encouragement has come from studies of CSF levels of the main metabolite of serotonin (see Figures 3 and 5)—5-HIAA (Table 10) (75,80,94). These results suggest that a subgroup may be defined by low 5-HIAA levels in CSF among depressed patients. These patients may be *either* unipolar or bipolar and are not readily separable by other clinical characteristics.

One intriguing proposal emerging from the work of Åsberg, Van Praag, Maas, and Goodwin and their colleagues is that low CSF levels of 5-HIAA may correspond with normal levels of urinary MHPG (serotonin-deficient or, in Maas' terminology, "type B" depression) and correlate with selective responsiveness to serotonin-enhancing agents such as precursor amino acids or agents active against serotonin uptake, including clomipramine or amitriptyline (96,104). Conversely, normal CSF levels of 5-HIAA and low levels of urinary excretion of MHPG (norepinephrine-deficient or "type A" depression) may define a group of endogenously depressed patients who respond preferentially to drugs that selectively enhance noradrenergic transmission (e.g., desipramine, imipramine)—an effect that may be predicted by an acute activating effect of a test dose of d-amphetamine (86). The ratio of patients with low versus normal CSF levels of 5-HIAA (ratio of types B:A) is about 1:4, based on limited available data (96).

Unfortunately, this approach may not be practical for routine clinical application, due again to the variance in the MHPG measurement, as well as the variance in 5-HIAA values (about 30%, or about the same as the mean difference between levels in antidepressant-responsive versus nonresponsive depressed patients), as well as the impracticality of routine lumbar punctures (80). Urinary assays of 5-HIAA have been found not to be a useful alternative (75,94). In addition, there is a suspicion that much of the apparent bimodality of distribution of CSF levels of 5-HIAA may be due to inexact matching of groups by sex (males tend to have lower values) (80). If a biologically and clinically meaningful subgroup were defined by such an approach (regardless of applicability to clinical practice), much more study would be required.

One other result of studies of metabolites in CSF is that there is now strong agreement (all of eight studies) that antidepressant treatment regularly leads to decreases of 5-HIAA (80), a result that accords well in theory with recent evidence that antidepressants may increase the functional sensitivity of central 5-HT receptors (Table 7; see also next chapter) (69). There is also weak evidence the ECT may lower levels of 5-HIAA in CSF (80), and MAO inhibitors, of course, directly prevent formation of this deaminated metabolite.

Several recent studies are pointing to new and imaginative approaches to the continuing search for clinical support of amine hypotheses in the major mood disorders. These depend on recent developments related to increased understanding of the role of aminergic receptors in the CNS. For example, there have been attempts to evaluate the status of aminergic receptors that are believed to be present in blood elements, such as leukocytes or platelets. There is evidence that the binding of the radiolabeled α_2 agonist, clonidine, to platelet membranes may be increased in depressed patients and decreased by antidepressant treatment (105), although the kinetics of binding underwent complex changes in this experiment and artifacts due to previous exposure to anti-depressants were not completely excluded.

In addition, it has recently been reported that plasma levels of cyclic-AMP are decreased in some depressed patients, which suggests diminished stimulation or sensitivity of β-adrenergic receptors in some tissues that may correlate with recent indications of a possible antidepressant effect of certain centrally active β-adrenergic agonists, such as salbutamol (albuterol) (106). The implication of altered sensitivity of α_2 autoreceptors in depression has been under consideration for some time (107). It has usually been inferred that increased activity of presynaptic receptors or autoreceptors would tend to diminish the output of norepinephrine into the synapse, and the finding of increased binding of clonidine in platelets of depressed patients appears to be in accord with that prediction (105).

It has also been suggested that antidepressant treatment may lead to reduced sensitivity of such autoreceptors, based on studies of the effects of desipramine on plasma MHPG levels in depressed patients (diminished lowering of MHPG by clonidine) (108). These results appear to be consistent with current views about the possible late anti-α_2 actions of antidepressants in the heart and brain (tending to increase release of norepinephrine), as is discussed in more detail in the next chapter.

Another new index of possible alteration of amine metabolism in depression is the finding of apparent reduction of the maximum velocity of uptake of serotonin by platelets prepared from the blood of depressed patients (109). If this result is valid, it seems counter to the concept of decreased availability of serotonin in the brain in depression. A corresponding observation is that the binding of tritiated imipramine, which is believed to bind at high affinity to serotonin transport sites in brain and other tissue, is decreased in membranes of platelets prepared from blood samples of depressed patients (110). This finding is not compelling, since there was more than 90% overlap of results between control and depressed subjects. Indeed, the risks of artifacts from experiments of this kind—due to recent exposure to antidepressant agents that have known potent interactions with the systems under study—are high.

In general, the status of findings concerning amine hypotheses in depressive disorders remains unsettled. There are repeated suggestions that decreased availability or action of monoamines might occur during depression, especially in manic-depressive or bipolar illnesses, although the evidence is neither strong nor consistent. It remains unproven that amine deficiency in the brain is either a necessary or sufficient basis for the occurrence of depression.

NEUROENDOCRINE FINDINGS

It has been known or suspected for many years that the regulation of hormone metabolism is altered in severe psychiatric illnesses. More recently, several specific abnormalities have been described that are apparently characteristic of severe depression (111–115). Some of these have been studied in the context of seeking metabolic signs of putative abnormalities of amine functions in the limbic system and hypothalamus that may lead to dyscontrol of the release of hormones from the anterior pituitary.

This approach has also encouraged clinical investigators to evaluate pathophysiologic features of depression for their own sake and without the necessity of supporting a preconceived body of theory. Simultaneously, there has also been increased interest in the clinical utility of endocrine measurements to be used as laboratory tests to aid in the diagnosis and treatment of patients. Several of the well-evaluated or still preliminary endocrine findings in depression and mania are summarized in Table 11, based on the reviews already cited (111–115) and studies cited below. Note that the table provides illustrative summaries and not an exhaustive review of every study reported.

The Hypothalamic-Pituitary-Adrenal Axis

It has been known for more than a decade that severe depression is associated with excessive secretion of cortisol from the adrenal cortex. Sachar and others applied the technique of 24-hour sampling of blood through an indwelling venous catheter to permit detection of ultradian "spikes" of release of cortisol and evaluation of their circadian rhythm (116). This approach revealed that in depression spikes were higher and more frequent and the normal day-night rhythm was less obvious. Although this markedly increased release of cortisol was at first thought to reflect psychotic disorganization in severe depression (111,116), Carroll and colleagues found that similarly agitated and disorganized schizophrenic subjects failed to show a similar high output of cortisol (117,118). More recently this group and several others have recommended replacement of simple measurements of cortisol levels in plasma or urine in favor of a dexamethasone suppression test (DST). This relatively simple diagnostic test has been under evaluation in many centers in the hope that it would be comparable in reliability and clinical utility to laboratory tests that are considered standard in medical practice and clinical pathology (115,119).

TABLE 11

Neuroendocrine Responses in Major Mood Disorders

Hormone	Change	UP vs. BP	Data Quality
Cortisol			
Basal	Increase	BP = UP	Good
Rise with ACTH	Increase	?	Good
Brain cortisol	Decrease	?	Weak
DST			
Depressed	Breakthrough	BP ≥ UP (?)	Very good
Manic or euthymic	Suppressed[a]	—	Good
ACTH level	Increased when DST is positive	?	Weak
Growth hormone			
Basal	None	—	Fair
Stimulated (by insulin or CA agonists)[b]	Decrease	UP > BP	Good
Thyroid-stimulating hormone (TSH)			
Basal	None	—	Fair
TRH			
Depressed	Decrease	UP ≥ BP (?)	Fair
Manic	Decrease	—	Fair
Prolactin			
Basal			
Mean	Decrease or no change	BP > UP	Fair
Rhythm	Diminished	BP = UP	Weak
DOPA (decrease)	Normal	—	Weak
Morphine (increase)	Less	BP = UP (?)	Fair
Luteinizing hormone			
Basal	Small decrease	UP = BP	Weak
Testosterone			
Basal	None	—	Weak

[a] Recent clinical experience suggests that some manic patients may also have a positive DST, but the evidence that DST normalizes with euthymia is good.

[b] Amphetamines, DOPA, clonidine, and desipramine have all been used as NE agonists.

The DST has been standardized as follows (115). The synthetic glucocorticoid is given in an oral dose of 1.0 mg (0.5 mg for children) at 11:00 or 11:30 p.m. on day 1. On day 2, plasma samples are collected at 4:00 and 11:00 p.m. or sometimes, for simplicity and convenience for outpatients, at 4:00 only. Normally, adrenal function is strongly suppressed by dexamethasone through hypothalamic-pituitary mechanisms that inhibit release of adrenocorticotropic hormone (ACTH) for more than 24 hours. In endogenous depressions, the suppressing effect is incomplete and short-lived. A criterion of 5 μg/dl (50 ng/ml) by transcortin protein binding assay (or somewhat less when more specific radioimmunoassay is used) has been established as a cut-off; above this level the DST is said to be *positive*. The use of the afternoon and evening samples can detect about 98% of all positive results, while the afternoon sample by itself finds about 79%; morning samples are reportedly less valuable, since they include a high proportion of low values of cortisol.

The DST and other biomedical measurements in depression, and in clinical pathology in general, are evaluated as to their *sensitivity* ("true" rate of positive test results in patients for whom the index diagnosis has been confirmed by another means, usually by clinical examination in depression) and *specificity* (rate of negative results in a comparison or control population). These and other measures of the reliability and potential clinical utility of medical tests are summarized in Table 12.

While the DST is evidently quite selective for major depressions (few false positive results, with a specificity in excess of 90%), there is increasing evidence (as it is applied under increasingly realistic field conditions in clinical studies) that its sensitivity is quite limited (120–125), currently averaging about 50%. A summary of recent studies that permit analysis of the sensitivity and specificity of the DST is provided in Table 13. To date, only about 4–6% of nonde-pressed subjects (most were normal or only mildly psychiatr-ically ill, or schizophrenic) have been reported to have a pos-itive DST, which yields, on average, a mean specificity of 94% (Table 13); the rate was also below 10% in a group of recuperating orthopedic patients (22). Yet there is a growing anecdotal impression that some severely agitated and dis-tressed psychiatric patients (and possibly some nonpsychia-tric patients), including an unknown proportion of manic and other acutely psychotic patients, may also yield positive DST results. Further critical studies are thus in order, particu-larly with patients who have disorders other than major depressions, so as to test the proposal that at least the spec-ificity of the DST in depression is quite high.

While the overall results with the DST so far are en-

TABLE 12

Evaluation of Biologic Tests in Medicine

Measure	Meaning
Sensitivity	Rate of positive tests among those suspected of diagnosis ("true" positive rate)
Specificity	Rate of negative tests in a control population ("true" negative rate)
Positive predictive value[a]	Rate of true positives to all positive tests
Negative predictive value	Rate of true negatives to all negative tests

[a] Also known as "predictive power" or "diagnostic confidence."

TABLE 13

Summary of Results of the DST in Depressed vs. Control Subjects

Study (N = 13)	Reference	Year	Sensitivity (%)	Specificity (%)
Carroll et al	118	1976	48	98
Brown et al	88	1979	40	100
Brown and Shuey	129	1980	50	94
Carroll et al	—[a]	1980	40	98
Holsboer et al	—[b]	1980	22	85
Nuller and Ostrounova	130	1980	69	91
Schlesser et al	127	1980	52	100
Carroll et al	114	1981	67	96
Amsterdam et al	—[c]	1982	26	85
Finklestein et al	22	1982	75	92
Poznanski et al	125	1982	56	89
Rush et al	119	1982	49	95
Targum et al	123	1982	33	100
Total ± SEM			48.2 ± 4.5	94.1 ± 1.5

Note: Conditions of testing varied among studies: outpatient samples and the use of single sampling times for the cortisol assay tended to reduce sensitivity. Finklestein et al tested depressed stroke patients; Poznanski et al evaluated children (for whom 0.5 mg of dexamethasone is preferred, versus 1.0 mg for adults); see the 1981–82 citations (115–133); specificity may be lower if manic and other acutely psychotic subjects are included in the comparison to depressed patients.

[a]Carroll BJ, Schroeder K, Greden JF et al: Plasma dexamethasone concentrations and cortisol suppression response in patients with endogenous depression. J Clin Endocrinol Metab 51:433–437, 1980.

[b]Holsboer F, Klein H, Bender W, Benkert O: Hypothalamic-pituitary-adrenal activity in a group of 100 heterogenic depressed patients: Diagnostic validity and biochemical aspects of the cortisol response to dexamethasone suppression. Prog. Neuropsychopharmacol (CINP Congress Suppl.): 180, 1980.

[c]Amsterdam JD, Winokur A, Caroff SN, Conn J: The dexamethasone suppression test in outpatients with primary affective disorder and healthy control subjects. Am J Psychiatry 139:287–291, 1982.

couraging, the limited sensitivity presents a problem in the use of the DST as a general screening test to aid in the diagnosis of depression—especially in cases that are not already obvious by clinical examination—and due to the degrading effect on positive predictive power of the test as the *prevalence* of the condition sought decreases. There are hopes that the DST might aid in the differential diagnosis of difficult cases, such as cases of dementia in the elderly, some of whom (sometimes diagnosed as having "pseudodementia" of depression) respond favorably to antidepressant therapy (126). Nevertheless, when the DST *is* positive, possible important clinical uses might follow, such as the prediction of response to treatment or prediction of the risk of relapse.

The test detects both unipolar and bipolar types of depression, although rates of positive DST tend to be somewhat higher for bipolar patients (who may be more homogeneous biologically), and a family history of a major mood disorder may increase the rate of positive tests up to 80–90% (115, 127, 128). On average, there are about 50% presumably false negative results with the DST (Table 13). Negative results may be relatively unusual in cases with strong clinical, descriptive, and family history evidence of major melancholic depressive illness—that is, in cases in which the diagnosis is least likely to be uncertain! Whether this impression is valid or not, at present a negative DST cannot be taken to exclude the diagnosis of major depression. Positive results can help to confirm cases of major depression, especially when the diagnosis is unclear on clinical grounds alone, but the decision to treat remains essentially a clinical one.

The result of the DST in depression is evidently not due to abnormal metabolism of dexamethasone or altered binding or elimination of cortisol, nor is it related in an important way to age (age accounts for only 2% of the variance)

(115,127). While there had been suggestions that severity of depression may contribute to a positive result on the DST, this is now thought not to be a controlling factor, although the more classically melancholic depressions also tend to be the most severe. Nevertheless, the DST has clearly distinguished between groups of patients with primary depressions and those with secondary depressions of well-matched severity (115). In addition, the correlation between severity of depression as assessed by standardized rating scales and 4:00 p.m. cortisol levels the day after a dose of dexamethasone is reportedly very weak (r = −0.20) (115). The use of DST under standardized conditions similar to those outlined above has recently been widely replicated in several American and European psychiatric centers in studies involving more than 1000 depressed patients (115–133).

Potential confusion in applying the DST can occur (115) during pregnancy or corticosteroid therapy, with the use of high doses of estrogens (ordinary menopausal replacement therapy and the use of contraceptive steroids are not a problem) or the use of reserpine or narcotics, and in the presence of Cushing's disease, uncontrolled diabetes, severe weight loss, serious medical illness, and some organic mental syndromes, as well as after stroke (22)—all of which may be associated with positive test results (and, sometimes, with depression!). Ordinary doses of antidepressants, lithium salts, and neuroleptics seem not to produce problems, while high doses of benzodiazepines and use of sedatives and anticonvulsants (which induce hepatic drug- and steroid-metabolizing enzymes) can all produce spurious positive test results.

While theory indicates that dexamethasone suppression in depression is due to dyscontrol of ACTH (corticotropin) release, there has been little direct evaluation of plasma ACTH in depression. There are two reports that basal plasma

ACTH levels were not elevated in depressed patients who had a positive DST result, so that peripheral (and perhaps adrenal) mechanisms should also be considered further, although the early escape from suppression by dexamethasone was found with respect to ACTH as well as to cortisol (122,131). It is suspected that norepinephrine and serotonin play important roles in the control of ACTH release at the level of the limbic system and hypothalamus. Nevertheless, the precise role of monoamines in the control of ACTH in humans remains unclear due to some pharmacologic effects in humans and lower primates that seem *not* to fit models derived from laboratory animals, which indicate an inhibitory control of corticotropin-releasing factor (CRF), a peptide hormone produced in the hypothalamus by α-noradrenergic or dopaminergic effects, and facilitation of CRF release by serotonin (112).

Dexamethasone suppression is clearly state dependent, since cortisol levels tend to fall with treatment and recovery and they are not elevated in recovery after depression (euthymia) (114,132). Several studies have attempted to correlate the DST with other biological measurements in depression (121–123), and others are currently under way. Also, provocative preliminary attempts to use the DST as a predictor of response to antidepressant treatment (129) or of risk of relapsing (132,133) have so far been inconclusive and require further study (115).

Other Neuroendocrine Responses

Other endocrinologic characteristics of depressed patients are less well evaluated than are cortisol and its suppression; highlights of these characteristics are summarized in Table 11. Growth hormone (GH) is known to be released by α-adrenergic, dopaminergic, and serotonergic agonists, but again comparisons between lower animals and primates are uncertain (112). Several laboratories have reported that, while basal levels of GH are normal in depressed patients, their response to some but not all adrenergic agonists is reported to be low (115). These state-dependent differences may differentiate patients with primary endogenous depression from neurotic patients and normal subjects, but so far they do not differentiate unipolar from bipolar mood disorders; mania has not been evaluated adequately.

Growth hormone responses to noradrenergic agonists that yield plasma levels below 4 ng/ml are reported to differentiate primary from secondary depressions fairly well in nearly a dozen studies, although low values have been found in about a third of normal subjects or patients who have secondary depressions. Nevertheless, a high value may rule out endogenous primary depression in 70–90% of cases (134). Among the problems associated with GH response tests in depression are invalidation by the HCAs and spurious results if a venous catheter is merely inserted or if the patient falls asleep during a test (115).

While most thyroid function tests are in the normal range in depression, several laboratories have reported that elevations of thyroid-stimulating hormone (TSH)—thyrotropin—by intravenous injections of the peptide thyrotropin-releasing hormone (TRH)—protirelin—are diminished in severe depression and possibly also in mania (113,135). Release of TRH from the hypothalamus may be stimulated by norepinephrine and dopamine and inhibited by serotonin but not by ACh (112). Results are conflicting, or very preliminary, as to whether the TRH-TSH test may help to differentiate unipolar from bipolar cases of depression (TSH responses may be slightly more blunted in unipolar illnesses) (136,137) or to separate mania and schizoaffective illness (which may be closely related to or even synonymous with manic-depressive illness) (11) from chronic schizophrenia, which reportedly is characterized by normal TSH responses to TRH (138). To some extent the TSH response may be confounded by interactions of high cortisol levels (115). A potentially important recent observation is that the blunted TSH response to TRH in primary unipolar depression may, to some extent, represent a trait since it persisted following recovery in 68% of a small group of patients (139), although in other cases the response has reverted to normal after clinical recovery (135).

In recent applications of the TRH-TSH test, intravenous doses of 0.5 mg of protirelin have usually been employed, and TSH has been assayed by radioimmunoassay at several points over the next one to two hours, with the patient at rest. The largest difference between basal levels of TSH and those found following injection of TRH is defined as the Δ TSH value. There is still some uncertainty as to the lowest value of Δ TSH to accept as a cut-off point: various laboratories recommend values below 7 or 5 micro-units (μU) per milliliter of serum. In recent reports, values below 7 μU/ml were found among 7% (140) to 12.5% (135) of normal subjects or patients with minor depressive illnesses, and in 0% (135) to 14% (141) of patients diagnosed as schizophrenic. At a value of 5 μU/ml or less, only 0–4% of schizophrenic patients were detected (135,141). Overall, in major depressions, a value below 7 μU/ml for TSH detects about 50% of cases, with a specificity of about 90% (135,140,141). By lowering the criterion level to only 5 μU/ml, the specificity can be increased to 96–100%, but the sensitivity drops to only 26–33% (135,141).

In addition to occasional positive results in apparently

mild depressions, the TSH response to TRH has also been found to be blunted in some cases of anorexia nervosa, in some recovered alcoholics, and during treatment with a lithium salt, as well as during treatment with corticosteroids (135). The prognostic value of an abnormally low TSH response remains unclear since the proportion of cases in which the change may be long-lasting (possibly a trait) is uncertain. The basis of this abnormality is evidently not identical to that of positive results of the DST, since only a minority of patients with a major depression have been found to have both abnormalities simultaneously (perhaps as few as 11–33%) (123,135).

In addition, there have been repeated attempts to demonstrate therapeutic efficacy in depression of thyroxin, TSH, or TRH as mood-elevating agents. These efforts have yielded mixed results that have not been consistently replicated, although a recent controlled study found beneficial effects among 75% of 12 patients with a major depression who initially responded poorly to amitriptyline or imipramine alone, but who then improved when 0.15 mg of triiodothyronine was added to their regimen daily for an additional three weeks (142).

Release of prolactin (PL) is known to be inhibited by dopamine and facilitated by serotonin (112), as well as by opiates (143). While there are relatively few studies of PL in depression, there are recent suggestions that bipolar depressed patients may have somewhat lower basal plasma levels of PL and a blunted release during sleep (144), and that depressed patients generally may have a blunted PL release in response to infusion of an opiate (143).

Thus, in summary, the evidence is increasingly compelling that many patients with severe depression have abnormalities of the regulation of release of cortisol or TSH. Curiously, the two abnormalities occur together in only a minority of patients investigated so far. While both phenomena are claimed to be fairly specific to depression (specificity is reportedly about 90% for both the DST and the TRH test, provided that cases of mania are excluded), their sensitivity is limited (only about 50% of cases diagnosed clinically are detected), especially when criteria are set so as to maximize the specificity of the tests.

The phenomenon of dexamethasone suppression is almost certainly a concomitant of the *state* of depression and may have some prognostic value in predicting a high risk of relapse if the test remains abnormal despite clinical improvement. Nevertheless, it has not been proved that the DST is a more reliable prognostic index than careful clinical evaluation. In addition, so far, improvement rates in response to an antidepressant have not been consistently greater in DST-positive than in DST-negative cases of severe depression. The blunted response of TSH to an infusion of TRH is an intriguing phenomenon, since some cases appear to remain abnormal even months after full clinical recovery. Why this pattern is not consistent (state dependent in some cases) is not clear.

While both of these rather well-evaluated endocrinologic markers of depression are of value in confirming a diagnosis and in the follow-up of patients who manifest the abnormality, their sensitivity of only about 50% severely limits their value in differential diagnosis or as a screening technique for cases that are not obvious on clinical examination.

NEUROPHYSIOLOGICAL FINDINGS

Patients with severe depression have altered sleep electroencephalographic (EEG) patterns, as might be anticipated in view of classic alterations in sleep behavior in depression. It was reported by Kupfer and Foster in the early 1970s that a key feature in severe depression is a shortened latency between falling asleep (even when sleep onset is delayed) and the start of the first period of rapid-eye-movement (REM), or dreaming, phases of sleep, as well as increased REM activity throughout the night (145). These characteristics can now be used successfully to differentiate primary endogenous depressions from secondary depressions associated with other medical or psychiatric illnesses, or from other forms of insomnia, in over 80% of cases (145–147). This observation has been replicated by several investigators and appears to rest on solid ground. Some typical values for changes in REM latency are summarized in Table 14.

The REM latency phenomenon does not seem to differentiate unipolar from bipolar depressions and has not yet been adequately evaluated in mania (which is technically dif-

TABLE 14
REM Sleep Latency in Psychiatric Disorders

Group	REM Latency (Min ± SEM)
Controls	109± 12
Schizophrenics	95± 12
Neurotics	87± 5
Unipolar depressives	45± 5 [a]
Bipolar manic-depressives (depressed)	43± 6 [a]

Note: Severe depression was associated with latency as short as 18 min. Schizoaffective patients were indistinguishable from manic-depressives (145,146).

[a] Significant at p < 0.05

ficult). Reduced REM latency is clearly state dependent and to some degree reflects the severity of depression. It has been reported that muscarinic ACh agonists can mimic the changes found in depression, i.e., shorten REM latency in normal subjects (147). Other pharmacologic observations include indications that initial REM latency per se does not help to predict responsiveness to antidepressant therapy. On the other hand, Kupfer and colleagues found that the degree of delay or suppression of REM onset during the first two nights following small test doses of an antidepressant such as amitriptyline (50 mg) predicted the clinical response to a month of antidepressant treatment (148) and correlated significantly with plasma levels of the drug but poorly with urinary excretion of MHPG (149). Further studies are under way in which several metabolic and hormonal variables are being evaluated along with sleep EEG patterns.

These studies on the tendency for REM sleep to occur earlier or to be increased in depression and for antidepressants to suppress or delay REM sleep (148–150) led to the hypothesis that REM suppression or other sleep-altering effects of antidepressant treatments may be an important clue to their mechanism of action (151). These concepts have been given further support by recent provocative claims of antidepressant effects of selective deprivation of REM sleep by deliberately awakening patients at the onset of REM periods (151) or, more paradoxically, by brief partial deprivation of all phases of sleep (152).

One other EEG characteristic that has been suggested by Buchsbaum and his colleagues to be capable of differentiating unipolar from bipolar cases of depression is the pattern of response of EEG potentials evoked by sensory stimuli of increasing intensity—the average evoked response (AER) test (153). Bipolar patients are said to tend to increase

EEG amplitudes with increasing stimulus intensity ("aug-menters"), while unipolar patients have an opposite re-sponse, at least at strong stimulus intensity ("reducers"). This test has not yet been widely evaluated by other investigators and its significance and possible utility remain unclear.

In general, EEG and sleep EEG (or polysomnography) techniques are not readily available in clinical practice but, for those who have access to clinical or research sleep labo-ratories, the REM latency test may be helpful in evaluating complex or confusing cases. Preliminary analysis of available data suggests that sleep EEG studies may perform at least as well in diagnosis as the DST or TRH test (Table 15).

OTHER APPROACHES

A large body of literature and clinical experience in the use of chemical assays of blood-drug levels of HCAs now exist to aid in providing optimal treatment regimens for depressed patients (155–157). The attempt to predict individual clinical responses to an HCA from blood levels of the drug or its major metabolites has not been highly successful. While trends have been reported among groups of patients given controlled, presumably adequate, doses of an antidepres-sant, the interindividual metabolic variance has been so high that it is difficult to state optimal blood levels for groups of patients (155,156).

Several HCAs have been found to provide measurable blood levels of the parent drug and its pharmacologically ac-tive, major N-demethylated metabolite in the case of tertiary amine antidepressants such as imipramine or amitriptyline. These agents yield variable total amounts in vivo of desipra-mine and nortriptyline, respectively. The total HCA levels are typically about 100–300 ng/ml of plasma or serum (Table

16), or about 10^{-6} molar; levels following treatment with secondary amine HCAs are usually somewhat lower than are the total levels of HCAs after treatment with the tertiary amine agents. Such concentrations of drug are adequate to account for most of the known pharmacologic actions of these agents discussed later; levels of free (unbound) drug are not known with accuracy (possibly 10–20% of total), nor is it clear whether only the free fraction is available to the brain, as is

TABLE 15

Examples of Performance of Some Biologic Tests in Depression

Test	Reference	Sensitivity (%)	Specificity (%)
REM sleep	119,147	64	86
Endocrine battery (DST, TRH, GnRH, ITT)	124	96	71
TRH plus DST	123	76	94
DST[a]		48	94
TRH	123,135,141	47	91
Urinary MHPG to predict response to maprotiline	100[b]	67	81
Plasma drug levels to predict response to imipramine	154	44	33

Note: Analyses include dexamethasone suppression test (DST) of cortisol secretion, elevation of thyroid-stimulating hormone (TSH) by thyrotropin-releasing hormone (TRH), release of luteinizing hormone (LH) and follicle-stimulating hormone (FSH) by gonadotropin-releasing hormone (GnRH), and an insulin-tolerance test (ITT) that included several hormone assays as well; MHPG assays in 24-hour urine samples; and gas-chromatographic assays of plasma imipramine and desipramine (which is the least promising test of the above samples for routine clinical use in guiding treatment).

[a] See Table 13.

[b] Others have not found supportive results (97,98).

sometimes supposed. Toxicity is commonly encountered
when blood levels of typical HCAs exceed 500 ng/ml.

A widely discussed concept has suggested that the demethylated (secondary amine) antidepressants, such as nortriptyline and perhaps desipramine, may have a biphasic relationship between blood level and clinical response. That is,
excessively high as well as low levels of the drug in plasma
have been reported to be associated with relatively poor
clinical outcome, although not necessarily with toxicity (155–
157). In contrast, the methylated (tertiary amine) antidepres-

TABLE 16

Pharmacokinetic Characteristics of Antidepressants in Humans

Drug	Amine Type	Half-Life (hr)	Typical Plasma Levels (ng/ml)
Imipramine	Secondary	16	150–300
Amoxapine	Secondary	8 + 30 [a]	?
Amitriptyline	Tertiary	30	100–250
Desipramine	Secondary	33	100–300
Doxepin	Tertiary	34	100–200
Maprotiline	Secondary	48	200–500
Nortriptyline	Secondary	52	50–150
Protriptyline	Secondary	126	100–200

Note: On overdose, elimination half-life may be somewhat longer than the approximate values listed. Amoxapine itself is rapidly (8 hr) metabolized to active ring-OH
products (30 hr). Higher levels of some secondary amine agents (notably nortriptyline and protriptyline) *may* be associated with a loss of efficacy. These agents are
strongly bound in plasma (>80%) and have high volumes of apparent distribution
(>10 L/kg), reflecting high lipid solubility and tissue binding

[a] Includes about 10–20% parent drug and 89–90% ring-hydroxylated products (8-
OH-amoxapine predominates in man over the 7-OH metabolite, which has loxa-
pine-like neuroleptic effects).

75

sants, such as amitriptyline and imipramine, have been reported to yield better clinical results as the levels of the parent drug plus its major demethylated metabolite rose, from about 100 to about 300 ng/ml. The latter relationship suggests that, if blood-drug assays are not readily available, it may be simpler to start with a tertiary amine agent and to increase doses gradually until the desired clinical effect is obtained or early signs of mild toxicity intervene. Although some data support this concept of biphasic versus monophasic response, it does not appear to be sufficiently strong as to have an important bearing on clinical decisions in the management of cases treated with either type of drug.

Commercial laboratories are making such blood-drug assays readily available for clinical application, yet their value remains unclear for the routine management of typical cases of depression, especially as their specificity and sensitivity as clinical tests are poor (Table 15) (154). Their clinical value may, however, be found in the evaluation of patients whose response is atypical, for example, a poor antidepressant response to presumably adequate doses of a medication after several weeks, or striking toxicity after a moderate dose of an antidepressant, or treatment of elderly or cardiac patients who may be at greater risk of toxicity with antidepressants.

An additional potential value of blood assays of antidepressant drug levels arises from striking correlations between drug levels and ratings of depression in individual patients (155). That is, while there are serious problems in seeking to define optimal blood levels for groups of patients, due to marked interindividual variations in drug metabolism, one may be able to define an approximately appropriate dose for an individual patient on the basis of his or her handling of a "test dose" of an antidepressant.

Thus, several groups have found very high correlations

(r > o.go) between plasma levels of an antidepressant at 24 hours after a single small test dose and those found after several weeks of treatment with a presumably therapeutic dose (158–160). It has even been proposed that one can predict the approximate daily requirement for a therapeutic dose on the basis of the blood-drug level obtained after the test dose (158, 159). An example of this kind of prediction is provided in Figure 6, which is based on results obtained with imipramine in depressed patients (160). Although this approach has not yet been widely applied in clinical management of patients, it might have some merit, especially for elderly or infirm patients in whom the risks of intoxication may be higher than usual.

An additional biological measurement that can be helpful in defining an effective dose of an antidepressant is the criterion of inhibition of blood platelet MAO activity. During treatment with phenelzine (Nardil), platelet MAO activity has been inhibited by more than 85% (161, 162). The observed correlation between strong inhibition of platelet MAO (mainly so-called type B in humans, as will be discussed later) and optimal clinical antidepressant effects have encouraged the use of larger doses of phenelzine (45–90 mg/day) than were common in the past (162). Whether similar correlations hold for other MAO inhibitors is not certain. Some preliminary data suggest that this approach may be feasible with isocarboxazid (Marplan) but probably not with tranylcypromine (Parnate), since it typically produces strong MAO inhibition at clinically ineffective doses (163), nor with the experimental agent clorgyline (only selective against type A MAO, which is not present in human platelets).

There have been surprisingly few studies aimed at evaluating catecholamine hypotheses by measuring cardiovascular responses to infusions of noradrenergic agonists. The few

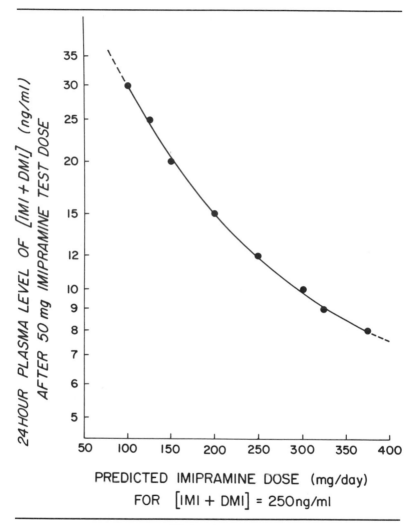

FIGURE 6

Prediction of Therapeutic Dose of Imipramine Based on Levels of Drug in Blood After a Small Test Dose

Note: These data are adapted from Brunswick and others (159), who evaluated depressed patients following a test dose of imipramine (50 mg orally). Based on the blood levels of imipramine plus desipramine found 24 hours later, and on the levels

that have been done have inconsistently suggested lesser (164) or greater (165) responses in depressed patients than in normal subjects; the possible influence of prior antidepressant treatment in these studies is unknown. There are several intriguing recent reports of altered indices of catecholamine receptor function in blood cells in depression as well. These include reports of diminished binding of ^{3}H-dihydroalprenolol (which labels β receptors) or of responses of isoproterenol-sensitive (β receptors) adenylate cyclase in platelets or leucocytes from depressed or manic patients (166,167).

These changes are believed to be state dependent and not to be artifacts of drug treatment (167), although they parallel decreases of β-adrenergic receptors induced by antidepressants in animal brain tissue by such treatment, as is discussed in the next chapter. Possible increases of α_2 binding sites in platelets from depressed patients (105) have already been discussed above. In addition, the binding of ^{3}H-imipramine to platelet membranes is reportedly diminished in depression (110,168). Although the significance of this form of "receptor" labeling is not yet clear, it may represent serotonin transport sites in cell membranes (110).

Still other theories based on studies of blood cells have also been reported. There have been repeated suggestions that erythrocytes (red blood cells) from bipolar manic-depressive patients are dissimilar to those of depressed or normal subjects in their ability to transport monovalent cations, notably Li^+, since a relatively high ratio of red blood cell to

---

obtained in patients followed for several weeks at presumably therapeutic doses, it was possible to estimate the dosage requirements so as to obtain blood-drug levels of 250 ng/ml, or a theoretically optimal therapeutic blood level of drug plus major metabolite. Based on these estimates, this figure expresses the predictive relationship between plasma drug level after the test dose and the expected therapeutic dosage requirement.

plasma Li^+ concentration (typically about 0.5) might predict clinical responses to lithium therapy (155,169) or since defective Na^+/Li^+ exchange processes might be inherited characteristics of manic-depressive patients and their first-degree relatives (enduring traits) (170). Unfortunately, these leads have not held up well in critical attempts at replication (155,171), nor is it certain that such changes are not due to previous treatment with lithium or other psychotropic agents.

One other lead concerning altered electrolyte metabolism in manic-depressive illness is the suggestion made by Coppen and his colleagues in the 1960s that "residual" (including intracellular) levels of sodium may be increased in both phases of the illness (172).

Another emerging strategy in biological research in depression is to measure a variety of physiological and biochemical changes in patients as a function of time of day, since it has long been recognized that altered circadian rhythmicity of mood and activity is a hallmark of the syndrome. Goodwin, Wehr, and colleagues have been using this approach intensively and found recently that depression is associated with temporal delays in the timing of the daily peak (acrophase) of body temperature, motor activity, and MHPG excretion; these peaks are delayed by perhaps 1.5 hours in depression and even longer (about 2 hours) in mania (102). The findings suggest that dyscontrol of circadian rhythms may be an essential feature of the pathophysiology of manic-depressive illness and that mania and depression may not be biological opposites. In addition, recent experimental therapeutic interventions aimed at altering the timing of sleep and activity in depressed patients (151,152,173) may be effective because of their interactions with altered regulation of daily bodily rhythms (173). The altered pattern of REM sleep in depression (145–150) suggests that abnormalities of shorter rhythms (ultradian) may also occur in major mood disorders.

For the future, there is a new class of technical advances that will almost certainly have a profound impact on research and clinical evaluations of the CNS in psychiatric and neurological illnesses. These include improved methods of evaluating cerebral blood flow in man, which are now beginning to suggest regionally selective decreases in depression (174). Thus far, computer-assisted x-ray tomography has only rarely been suggestive of subtle deviations in the ratio of ventricular to cortical mass in manic-depressive illness, although such deviations have been reported to occur in some schizophrenics (175), but still newer scanning methods are starting to emerge. These include methods for evaluating regional differences in the rate of glucose utilization, as well as other applications of positron-emission tomography and the use of nuclear magnetic resonance scanning methods (176–178). These new computer-analyzed techniques promise to revolutionize the clinical investigation of abnormal structure and function of the intact human brain.

CONCLUSIONS

The material reviewed here makes it clear that remarkable advances have been made in the application of biomedical methods to the evaluation of patients who have severe depressive and manic-depressive illnesses. There has been a trend away from attempts to support or refute biological hypotheses derived inductively from a partial understanding of the effects of psychotropic drugs and toward a more neutral and descriptive approach. This approach has provided powerful and compelling support for genetic and metabolic char-

TABLE 17

Clinical Features of Bipolar and Nonbipolar Depressive Illnesses

Feature	Bipolar	Nonbipolar
Mania, hypomania	+ + + +	0
Family history of mania or hypomania	+ + +	+ +
Mood switches	+ + + +	0
Sex ratio (female:male)	1.0	2.0
Median onset (years)	26	40
Five or more episodes (%)	18	6
Social class	Higher	Lower
Marital status	Married (discord)	Unmarried
Recent life stresses	+	+
Personality traits	Obsessive (?)	"Neurotic" (?)
Psychomotor retardation	+ +	+
Insomnia	+ + +	+ + +
Hypersomnia	+ +	+
Diurnal changes	+ + +	+ +
Agitation	+	+ + +
Anger in depression	+	+ + +
Somatic or neurotic symptoms	+	+ + +
Reduced REM sleep latency	+ +	+ +
Positive DST	+ +	+
Low urinary MHPG excretion	+	+/0
Average evoked EEG response	Augmentation (?)	Reduction (?)
Lithium as antidepressant	Probable	Uncertain
Prophylaxis	Lithium salts	Antidepressants

Note: This summary remains general and tentative as additional research data become available, as is discussed in the text. Note that risk rates in first-degree relatives have been more similar in families of bipolar and nonbipolar index patients in more recent studies, especially those in which nonbipolar cases have involved severe (melancholic) depression and family history has been obtained "blindly" and by direct examination or interview. Symbols represent: 0 = not found, + = weakly or variably associated, + + = moderately associated, + + + = typical feature, + + + + = strongly associated.

acterization of the major depressive syndromes and of their bipolar and nonbipolar (unipolar) variants. A summary of these characteristics is provided in Table 17. In addition, biological strategies have helped considerably to sharpen our ability to provide more nearly optimal application of available, though imperfect, antidepressant, antimanic, and mood-stabilizing medical therapies as improved treatments are being sought.

A general criticism of the field is that the practical application of some of the better clinical tests has been remarkably slow (74,179,180). Some (notably the DST and blood-antidepressant assays), while perhaps of questionable status for commercialization and routine clinical use, are at the very least interesting research methods worthy of broader field trials in clinical practice. Other endocrine measures and the REM latency test can be applied almost routinely in advanced treatment and academic centers. It is especially remarkable that more cross-validation among tests and clinical data in the same patients at the same time has made slow progress so far.

An additional recent development, which is beyond the scope of the present discussion, is the undertaking of objective testing of the efficacy of psychosocial treatments of mood disorders (181,182) and thoughtful attempts to integrate biomedical and psychosocial approaches (183,184).

3

Recent
Advances in
Antidepressant
Pharmacology

Since the appearance of the MAO inhibitors in the early 1950s and the phenothiazine analogs imipramine and its congeners in the late 1950s and early 1960s, there have been very few new antidepressant drugs in the United States, and the benefits and problems of most are remarkably similar to those of imipramine. The United States has been particularly slow in accepting many drugs long in clinical use in England and Europe, some of which, if not more effective, may be less toxic than older drugs. The recent addition of three new agents in the United States within the past three years (amoxapine, maprotiline, and trimipramine) raises our complement of imipramine-like or typical heterocyclic antidepressants (formerly called tricyclic antidepressants) to nine (Figure 7).

The formulations and doses of these HCAs are provided in Table 18; some of their pharmacokinetic characteristics were presented above (Table 16). Another HCA that has *atypical* pharmacologic characteristics, trazodone, has also been introduced recently. Clomipramine (3-chloro-imipramine, Anafranil) is also in use in Europe and Canada and is in advanced clinical trials in the United States. Three MAO

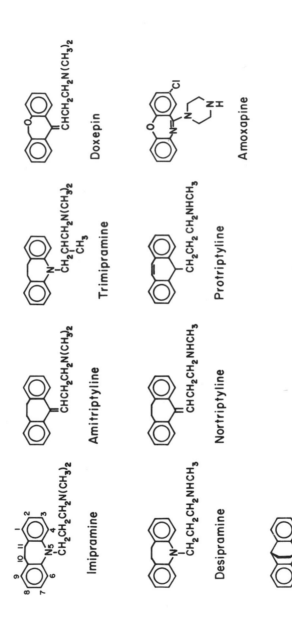

Imipramine

Amitriptyline

Trimipramine

Doxepin

Desipramine

Nortriptyline

Protriptyline

Amoxapine

Maprotiline

86

FIGURE 7

Structure of Typical Heterocyclic Antidepressants Currently Available in the United States

Note: These nine agents have many pharmacologic characteristics in common with the original member of the series, imipramine, including an ability to interfere with the reuptake-inactivation of monoamines, especially norepinephrine. Trimipramine may be less active than other agents against norepinephrine uptake; doxepin is only slightly less active in clinically effective doses, and both may form desmethylated metabolites, which should be active. Amoxapine is the desmethyl derivative of a typical antipsychotic agent, loxapine, and has some neuroleptic-like as well as antidepressant properties, including antagonism of dopamine receptors, as well as ability to inhibit uptake of norepinephrine.

TABLE 18

Antidepressant Drugs: Preparations, Dosage Forms, and Dosages

Nonproprietary Name	Trade Names	Dosage Forms [a]	Daily Dose (mg) Usual	Daily Dose (mg) Extreme [b]
Heterocyclics				
Imipramine HCl[c]	Antipress, Imavate, Janimine, Presamine, SK-Pramine, Tofranil	T: 10, 25, 50 mg A: 25 mg/2ml	100–200	30–300
Amitriptyline HCl[c]	Amitril, Elavil, Endep	T: 10, 25, 50, 75, 100, 150 mg V: 10 mg/ml in 10 ml	75–200	50–300
(±)Trimipramine maleate[d]	Surmontil	C: 25, 50 mg	75–150	25–300
Doxepin HCl	Adapin, Curetin, Sinequan	C: 10, 25, 50, 75, 100, 150 mg S: 10 mg/ml	75–100	25–300
Desipramine HCl	Norpramin, Pertofrane	C: 25, 50 mg T: 25, 50, 75, 100, 150 mg	100–200	25–300
Nortriptyline HCl	Aventyl, Pamelor	C: 10, 25 mg S: 10 mg/5 ml	75–150[e]	20–150
Protriptyline HCl	Vivactyl	T: 5, 10 mg	15–40	10–60
Maprotiline HCl	Ludiomil	T: 25, 50 mg	100–150	25–300
Amoxapine HCl[f]	Asendin	T: 50, 100, 150 mg	200–300	50–600

88

Atypical antidepressants				
Trazodone HCl	Desyrel	T: 50, 100 mg	150–250	50–600
Alprazolam[g]	Xanax	T: 0.25, 0.5, 1.0 mg	—	—
MAO inhibitors				
Isocarboxazid	Marplan	T: 10 mg	10–40	10–60
Phenelzine sulfate	Nardil	T: 15 mg	15–60	15–90
Tranylcypromine sulfate	Parnate	T: 10 mg	20–30	10–40

[a] T = tablet; C = capsule; V = vial for intramuscular injection; A = ampul for intramuscular injection; S = oral solution or concentrate.

[b] Extreme doses are for very young and elderly patients (low doses) and for hospital use (high doses) in severe or treatment-resistant depression. In addition, due to the long biological half-life of MAO inhibition, smaller doses of MAO inhibitors may suffice after several days or weeks of treatment.

[c] Imipramine is also available as the pamoate (Tofranil-PM) in capsules containing 75, 100, 125, or 150 mg of the drug, but its advantages over the hydrochloride are not established. Amitriptyline hydrochloride is also available mixed with fixed doses of perphenazine in tablets containing 2/10, 4/10, 2/25, 4/25, or 4/50 mg of perphenazine/amitriptyline (Etrafon, Triavil) and mixed with chlordiazepoxide in tablets containing 5/12.5 mg of chlordiazepoxide/amitriptyline (Limbitrol).

[d] (±) = Racemic mixture of optical isomers.

[e] Although the usually recommended maximum daily dose is 100 mg, recent evidence indicates that many patients have relatively low concentrations in plasma and inferior clinical responses unless doses exceed 100 mg, while a few may have an excessive amount in doses above 150 mg/day.

[f] Amoxapine (nor-loxapine) may also have neuroleptic-like activity.

[g] Alprazolam, a triazolo-benzodiazepine, shares many pharmacologic properties with other anxiolytic benzodiazepines and has recently been approved for the treatment of anxiety; while somewhat higher doses may also provide useful antidepressant effects, based on several studies, this is not an approved indication at this time, and an antidepressant dose is not established.

inhibitors are also in current use (isocarboxazid, Marplan; phenelzine, Nardil; and tranylcypromine, Parnate). The U.S. Food and Drug Administration has approved the use of thioridazine for some forms of anxious depression, and other neuroleptics are common adjunctive agents in severe, agitated, or psychotic depression. ECT is still used selectively in severe depression. There are also broadening indications for the use of lithium salts. Thus, many effective and acceptably safe medical treatments are now available for depression and allied mood disorders (6–9, 179, 180).

In addition, the past decade has led to impressive advances in understanding of the nosology, description, genetics, and clinical biology of the mood disorders, all of which promise to contribute to more rational clinical evaluation and use of antidepressant and mood-stabilizing treatments. The present discussion, which is limited to recent developments in the discovery and evaluation of antidepressant chemicals, grows out of and complements the biomedical approach to depressive illnesses.

HOW DO ANTIDEPRESSANTS WORK?

The short answer to the difficult question of how antidepressants work is that no one knows. Since so little is known about the biological basis of depression itself, it may not yet be possible to know. The pharmacologic work summarized in this chapter is almost certainly biased by the rediscovery of more and more agents that block the uptake of norepinephrine, and some that block the uptake of serotonin, and by the still uncertain clinical status of the more provocatively "atypical" new agents that do not block amine uptake sites or receptors. While sustained norepinephrine-potentiating effects due to the blocking of uptake may contribute to the actions of many antidepressants, this is not a universal feature of all antidepressants, especially not of the newer atypical antidepressants. Since it may be possible to obtain useful antidepressant effects by more than one mechanism and since there are almost certainly several biologically dissimilar varieties of depression (74), it may not be reasonable to seek common actions for all antidepressants.

Nevertheless, some promising leads have come from evaluations of β-adrenergic and 5-HT$_2$ receptors, which appear to have a remarkably broad range of positive findings across many classes of agents. In addition, there are provocative findings concerning gradual increases of physiologic sensitivity to serotonin or diminishing sensitivity of presynaptic α_2-adrenergic receptors, which may increase the release of norepinephrine in the brain. It is difficult to conclude that the temporary and reversible loss of sensitivity of β-adrenergic receptors itself is therapeutic. It also remains uncertain how such receptors contribute to the function of the CNS and how they contribute to homeostatic responses to foreign chemical agents. A summary of the reported effects of antidepressants is provided in Table 19.

The Process of Developing Antidepressants

The currently available antidepressants are almost all remarkably similar in their pharmacology, toxicology, and spectrum of clinical utility. To a large extent, as with antipsychotic agents, this outcome reflects the limitations of pharmacologic theory and pharmaceutical practice in drug development. Our current, partial understanding of the actions of antidepressants continues to be dominated by monoamine neurotransmitter-based theories and hypotheses concerning the pathophysiology of depression—both of which are almost certainly oversimplified (179,180). Intriguing new leads to common pharmacodynamic features of old and some unusual new antidepressants are highlighted below. However, the prediction of antidepressant activity still remains closely tied to screening for evidence in laboratory animals or in vitro of catecholamine enhancement (such as ability to reverse behavioral effects of reserpine or other amine-de-

TABLE 19

Summary of Actions of Heterocyclic Antidepressants

Time Base	Action
Acute (hours)	Block uptake of NE $\geq$ 5-HT (except iprindole and a few other atypical agents) but not DA
	Reduce synthesis or turnover of NE or 5-HT
	Reduce firing rates of NE or 5-HT neurons
	Block 5-HT, ACh (muscarinic), NE (α_1), and histamine ($H_1 > H_2$) receptors (inversely with potency)
Late (weeks)	Block of amine uptake continues
	Return of turnover and firing rates
	Decrease NE (β) and (α_2, presynaptic) receptor sensitivity
	Increase NE release (α_2 effect?)
	Probably no change or some increase in NE (α_1) receptor sensitivity
	Uncertain effects of 5-HT receptors (increased physiologic responses but decreased binding to 5-HT$_2$ and perhaps to 5-HT$_1$ sites)
	No change or some increase in muscarinic ACh receptors
	No change in DA receptor binding, but possible increase in presynaptic DA receptor function to increase DA release

pleting agents, or to block the uptake of norepinephrine into isolated nerve endings).

More recently, increased attention has also been given to drugs that selectively block the uptake (inactivation) of serotonin and those with low antimuscarinic (anti-ACh) activity. Of more than 75 currently experimental antidepressants, about half are structural analogs of imipramine or are known to be inhibitors of norepinephrine uptake. Many of these represent minor chemical alterations of older compounds, including three of the new but typical HCAs mentioned above (see Figure 7). The close interdependence of theories of drug action and methods for their development may thus have contributed to the proliferation of many "me-too" drugs and to a still narrowly focused and incomplete understanding of the mechanisms by which antidepressant effects occur.

Newer Antidepressants

Of the many experimental agents, at least a dozen are already in clinical use in Europe and elsewhere. Most are pharmacologically similar to imipramine-like HCAs used in the United States; a few, such as iprindole, mianserin, and trazodone, are intriguing because their action mechanisms are obscure, and trazodone has recently been introduced into American medical practice (185–189) (the structures of these and several other new atypical or experimental antidepressants are shown in Figure 8). These atypical antidepressants are neither MAO inhibitors (virtually no new HCAs are) nor blockers of the uptake of norepinephrine, serotonin, or dopamine. Mianserin and iprindole have recently been suggested to subtly modify the release of norepinephrine, and trazodone may have some serotonin-uptake blocking action. A large number of agents, chemically similar to imipramine or not, have strong and sometimes highly selective effects on the uptake of norepinephrine. Effects against amine uptake in vitro are summarized in Table 20. Among the newer blockers of norepinephrine uptake (in rank order by in vivo potency), tandamine, nisoxetine, maprotiline, and viloxazine are highly selective in that they are 20 to 2000 times weaker against serotonin and virtually inactive against dopamine uptake (190–195).

The experimental agents fluoxetine and its congeners are potent and selective blockers of serotonin uptake. Several of these are undergoing clinical trials and may have useful antidepressant or antianxiety effects (195). Clomipramine is also a potent antagonist of serotonin uptake (and norepinephrine uptake). Whether facilitation of serotonin neurotransmission can account for their actions is unknown. Clearly, most currently used HCAs are poor blockers of serotonin uptake (see Table 20).

A more general question is whether blockade of uptake of monoamines (notably norepinephrine) is crucial for antidepressant action, as has often been inferred in the past. Some potent blockers of norepinephrine uptake are not effective antidepressants, but these do usually have short-lasting stimulant actions in humans. It may be that the rapid psychomotor excitatory effects of stimulants are mediated by their dopamine-enhancing actions and that these effects, which typically induce or worsen agitation, may limit their usefulness in depression.

One interesting generalization concerning amine uptake is that demethylated antidepressants, such as protriptyline, desipramine, and nortriptyline, are more potent against the uptake of norepinephrine than that of serotonin. In addition, N-demethylation of some antipsychotic drugs may yield mood-elevating products; an example is the new antidepres-

TABLE 20

In Vitro Inhibition of Uptake of Labeled Amines by Brain Tissue

Drug	Potency (IC_{50}, $n\,M$)[a] NE	5-HT	DA	Potency Ratio (NE:5-HT)
Protriptyline	2	1,600	5,200	800
Desipramine	2	2,000	15,000	1,000
Nomifensine	7	11,300	60	1,600
Nisoxetine	8	200	2,900	25
Maprotiline	20	24,000	9,300	1,200
Amoxapine[b]	23	566	—	25
Nortriptyline	30	1,400	5,300	6.7
Imipramine	60	490	15,600	7.3
Amitriptyline	130	300	6,200	3.5
Clomipramine	160	30	5,000	0.2
Doxepin	320	3,400	7,700	10.6
Fluoxetine	740	270	12,000	0.4
Mianserin	810	37,500	19,000	46.3
Viloxazine	1,400	64,000	56,000	45.7
Butriptyline	1,700	10,000	5,200	5.9
Iprindole	3,500	44,000	11,000	12.6
Trimipramine	4,400	5,400	6,700	1.2
Trazodone	>100,000	760	>100,000	>100
d-Amphetamine	78	21,000	280	270
l-Amphetamine	150	77,000	1,300	500
Cocaine	126	850	400	6.7
Methylphenidate	200	81,000	700	400
Benztropine	450	14,000	425	30
Chlorpromazine	150	10,000	12,000	66.7
Thioridazine	4,000	5,500	3,500	1.4

Note: Data are pooled for isolated nerve endings (synaptosomes) of rat forebrain (NE, DA, 5-HT) and mouse heart tissue (metaraminol as a model of NE) (190–195).

[a] The half maximally effective inhibitory drug concentration.

[b] Both 7-OH and 8-OH amoxapine had similar activity against NE and 5-HT uptake.

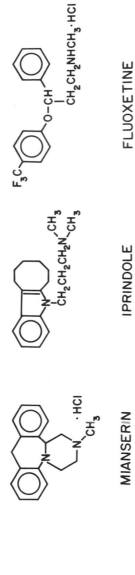

FLUOXETINE

S-ADENOSYLMETHIONINE

IPRINDOLE

ALPRAZOLAM

MIANSERIN

TRAZODONE

96

FIGURE 8

Structure of Atypical Heterocyclic Antidepressants

Note: These selected examples of new or experimental agents are distinguished from the more typical imipramine-like agents of Figure 7 by having little activity against uptake of monoamines (mianserin has some activity against uptake of norepinephrine; the others are virtually inactive). Alprazolam is now in use as an antianxiety agent in low doses but may be antidepressant in higher doses (4–8 mg/day). Trazodone has recently been released as the first atypical antidepressant in the United States (see also Table 18).

97

sant amoxapine (nor-loxapine), a selective blocker of the up-take of norepinephrine (191,196).

Still other classes of new antidepressants include tria-zolo-benzodiazepines (analogs of diazepam), notably alprazo-lam (Xanax), which has recently been released for clinical use in the United States as an antianxiety agent in low doses and may have useful antidepressant effects, especially in neurotic outpatients, in somewhat higher doses. Yet another unexpected finding is reported antidepressant effects of the natural metabolite, S-adenosylmethionine, which is in clini-cal use in Europe.

Selective Inhibitors of Monoamine Oxidase (MAO)

Interest in MAO inhibitors has increased following more than a decade of some reluctance to employ them in depres-sion, due to reports of severe toxic effects and sometimes dangerous interactions with other agents, as well as gener-ally unfavorable results in their placebo-controlled clinical trials. The recent change stems, in part, from demonstra-tions of results similar to those of standard HCAs with doses of phenelzine high enough (60–75 or even 90 mg/day) to in-hibit blood platelet MAO activity by more than 85% (161,162) and by growing evidence that MAO inhibitors may have util-ity in treating neuropsychiatric disorders other than depres-sions. The most commonly used antidepressant MAO inhib-itors in the United States are phenelzine and tranylcypromine (Figure 9).

More selective MAO inhibitors now under study are ca-pable of increasing brain levels of norepinephrine or seroto-nin (by inhibition of MAO type A) (197,198). An example of this type of inhibitor is clorgyline (Figure 10). An inhibitor

98

selective for MAO type B, deprenyl, is also known and is selective against deamination of phenethylamine and benzylamine. Tyramine is a substrate for MAO types A and B, and human gut is especially rich in MAO-A (as is the skin, while human platelets contain MAO-B activity). There is some evidence that the most extensively evaluated inhibitor selective

HYDRAZINE

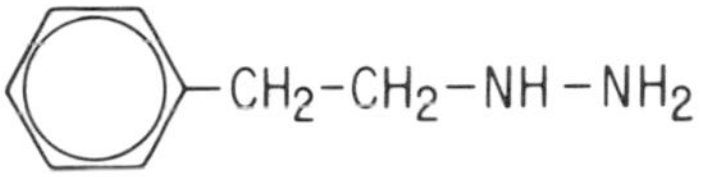

Phenelzine (Nardil)

NON-HYDRAZINE

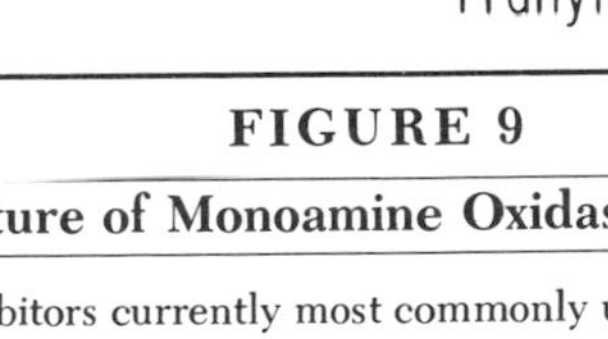

Tranylcypromine (Parnate)

FIGURE 9
Structure of Monoamine Oxidase Inhibitors

Note: The MAO inhibitors currently most commonly used as antidepressants in the United States are phenelzine (Nardil), a hydrazine compound, and tranylcypromine, an amphetamine-like nonhydrazine that is somewhat more potent; both are effective antidepressants when given in adequate doses. Isocarboxazid (Marplan) is also available but is not as commonly used at present. Other agents with MAO-inhibitory properties are also in clinical use for their antihypertensive (e.g., pargyline), antibiotic (furoxone), or antitumor (matulane) properties.

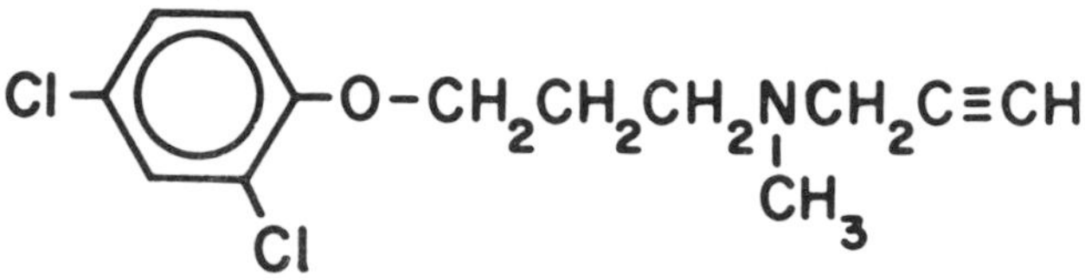

Clorgyline (A:B = 42)

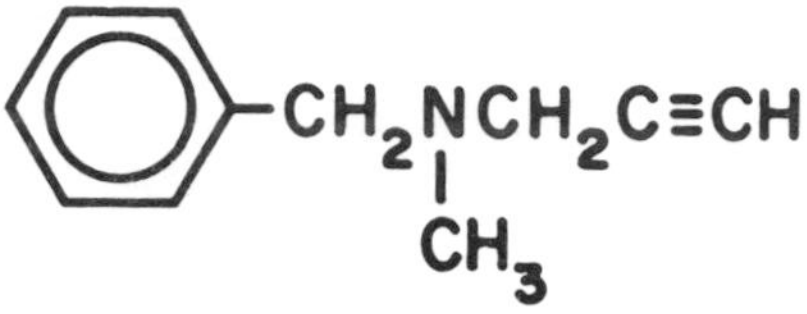

Pargyline (B:A = 15)

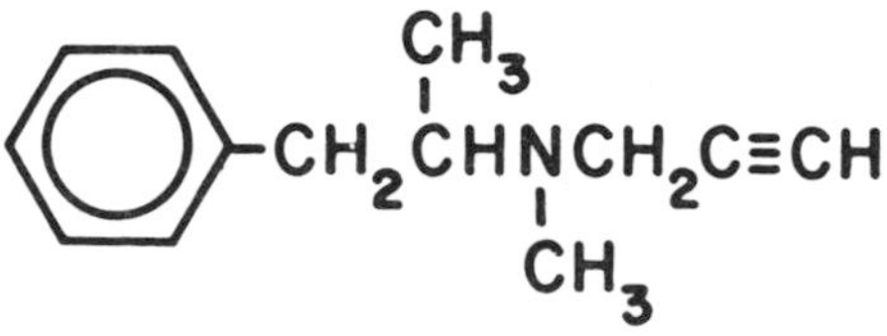

Deprenyl (B:A = 125)

FIGURE 10

Structure of Propargylamine MAO Inhibitors

Note: These agents are all believed to bind irreversibly to monoamine oxidase (MAO) after activation by the enzyme to act as "suicide inhibitors" of the enzyme. Pargyline is used as an antihypertensive agent, but is also antidepressant; it is somewhat selective for type B MAO activity, while the analogs clorgyline and deprenyl are selective for types A and B, respectively (selectivity ratios are in parentheses).

for MAO-B, deprenyl, may be safer in respect to hypertensive reactions due to tyramine in foods, although it appears to be less effective than other agents in depression (199). Preliminary clinical data suggest that the selective MAO-A inhibitor, clorgyline, is a more promising antidepressant; its use has been associated with improvement rates of 72–88% .and apparent safety (197). It is interesting to note that phenelzine, in clinical doses, is also relatively selective against MAO-A, while the other clinically available MAO inhibitor antidepressants, isocarboxazid and tranylcypromine, are 5 to 10 times less so (Table 21).

TABLE 21

Selectivity of MAO Inhibitors In Vivo

Drug	Typical Daily Dose (mg/kg)	ED_{50} (mg/kg)[a] 5-HT (A)	PEA (B)	Relative Anti-A Potency
Clorgyline	0.5	1	42	42
Harmine	—	10	>100	>10
Phenelzine	1.0	2.5	14.5	5.8
Isocarboxazid	0.5	2.5	2.1	0.8
Tranylcypromine	0.5	0.59	0.24	0.4
Pargyline	1.5	8.8	0.6	0.07
Deprenyl	1.5	50	0.4	0.008

Note: Selective substrates: MAO-A: 5-HT, MAO-B: phenethylamine (PEA); in vitro potency ratios were similar or showed even stronger differences in substrate preference. Data adapted from Maxwell and White (198), based on in vivo pretreatment of rat. Note that, of currently available MAO inhibitors, phenelzine is the most selective against MAO-A activity.

[a] The half maximally effective dose.

CLINICAL ASSESSMENT OF NEW ANTIDEPRESSANTS

Antidepressant drugs of the imipramine type are useful but imperfect antidepressants. They are surprisingly limited in efficacy. Typically, improvement rates in controlled trials of antidepressants in various forms of depression have averaged about 66–75%, while placebo response rates after about a month of treatment are often in the range of 20–40% and eventual spontaneous remission is the rule. Older HCAs produced results superior to placebo in only 64–71% of 85 controlled trials, and MAO inhibitors (prior to routine use of high doses) produced superior results in only 61% of their early controlled trials (6–9,200–202). While it is widely held that more severe depressions with clear biological signs are most likely to respond favorably, it may simply be easier to demonstrate a drug-placebo difference in sicker patients who have such clear biological signs. Newer antidepressants have so far *not* proved to be more effective than older agents in mild or severe depression, although newer atypical agents may be less toxic.

A paradoxical consequence of the partial success of available antidepressants is that rigorously controlled therapeutic trials are increasingly difficult to conduct, especially with severely ill patients. Inclusion of an inactive placebo condition or group (deliberately delaying treatment) is increasingly difficult to justify ethically. Moreover, many patients who were formerly seen in psychiatric centers and were available for experimental therapeutic studies are now treated by primary-care physicians. Nevertheless, the extraordinarily high prevalence rates of mood disorders (expectancy rates of 10% or more) support clinical and commercial interest in the development and testing of new antidepressant candidates. Many studies have made compromises by including less severely ill patients and large proportions of outpatients. Most studies of depression also rely on "drug A versus drug B" designs without the benefit of a placebo group to rule out false conclusions that would equate "not different from" with "as good as" the comparison treatment. Limitations of many studies that purport to demonstrate clinical antidepressant efficacy of newer agents have recently received comment elsewhere (72,185,187,196,202–209).

Typical examples are provided by reviews of outcome studies with amoxapine (196,204), trimipramine (208), maprotiline (205–207), and trazodone (188). Amoxapine was apparently found to be "as good as" imipramine or amitriptyline in 14 drug-comparison studies, but results were equivocal in at least one of only seven placebo-controlled studies in depression. In 14 studies involving hospitalized patients, maprotiline equalled comparison agents 86% of the time, and gave superior results in 14% of studies, but no placebo comparisons were reported. Trazodone outperformed a placebo in 75% of 12 controlled studies and did as well as a standard antidepressant in all of 21 comparisons reported recently (188). Similar results were found with trimipramine (208) and with other agents (207). But, again, few studies of severely ill patients are to be found, and only 20% of studies with some drugs included a placebo condition (207). In a review of still other studies involving several newer agents in more heterogeneous groups of patients, improvement rates among patients *within* studies ranged from 75% to only 10%, while standard agents such as imipramine yielded rates of 60–80% (187), as expected from the older literature (199,200).

Generally, the quality of improvement with new agents has been similar to that observed with older agents. Studies of amoxapine (196,204), trimipramine (208), and maprotiline

(205,206) initially suggested that the onset of beneficial effects might be somewhat faster than with standard comparison drugs, but this impression has not been sustained. Moreover, the supposedly inevitable two- to three-week delay in antidepressant effect of older agents may be exaggerated, since several studies using rapidly increasing doses in patients likely to respond have found antidepressant effects within a week (202), and early beneficial effects on sleep are routine. Actual *recovery* in depression may be limited in speed by the natural history and pathophysiology of the illness rather than by the effects of drugs.

A very serious question about newer antidepressants, especially the serotonin enhancers and the atypical group discussed above, is whether a significant proportion of their apparent effects may be due to anxiolytic actions or sedation in the many neurotic and anxious outpatients entered into their clinical trials. This question is an old one, since anxiolytic actions may contribute to supposed antidepressant effects of such neuroleptics as chlorpromazine and, more specifically, thioridazine, mesoridazine, thiothixene, and molindone, about which this question has been raised recently (184). The close similarity of loxapine and amoxapine (nor-loxapine) or trimipramine to phenothiazines, and of alprazolam to diazepam and other benzodiazepines, should also be considered in this context (see Figures 7 and 8). Some evidence concerning iprindole, however, suggests that it may even be less anxiolytic than imipramine (209).

Toxicity of Antidepressants

At least as important as the limitations of efficacy of available MAO inhibitors and HCAs are their toxic effects at therapeutic and excessive doses. The limited therapeutic index of available antidepressants—ratio of lethal or toxic to effective doses, as reflected in the potential lethality of even two weeks' supply (Table 18) or of blood-drug levels perhaps only five times therapeutic levels (Table 16)—is well known. Several of the newer atypical agents appear to lack strong effects on amine uptake mechanisms and receptors, including norepinephrine uptake sites or receptors and muscarinic acetylcholine receptors, and have a possibly corresponding lack of cardiac, visceral-autonomic, and cerebral toxicity. Nevertheless, most of the *typical* antidepressants recently introduced into American practice do not seem to be markedly less toxic than imipramine and its older congeners (Figure 7).

Aspects of antidepressant toxicity have been reviewed recently (206,210,211). A tentative rank-ordering for cardiovascular toxicity (tachycardia, hypotension, and quinidine-like cardiac depressant effects) goes from amitriptyline (at the worst) to imipramine and clomipramine, to doxepin, maprotiline, and dothiepin, to the serotonin-uptake blockers (fluoxetine and its congeners) or atypical agents (trazodone and alprazolam, as well as mianserin, iprindole, and others not yet available in the United States). Similar impressions derive from physiological studies of cardiovascular function and estimates of lethal doses in laboratory animals (206). Seizure threshold may be lowered by imipramine, clomipramine, maprotiline, and possibly amoxapine much more than by nomifensine and MAO inhibitors (which may actually have anticonvulsant actions) (162).

Before turning to further comments on the clinical use of antidepressant agents and needs for further research, it may help to summarize what is known about the actions of older and newer antidepressants on brain function.

Traditional Actions of HCAs in Amine Uptake

It has been known since the work of Axelrod and his colleagues in the early 1960s (212) that imipramine and other typical HCAs block the inactivation of norepinephrine by reuptake or transport at adrenergic nerve terminals in the peripheral, sympathetic, and central nervous systems (see Table 20). Many studies have added to the evaluation of this phenomenon and extended it to measurements of the transport of other monoamine neurotransmitters of the CNS, particularly serotonin. Potency values—the half maximally effective inhibitory drug concentrations (IC_{50})—for individual drugs have varied considerably among laboratories, and comparisons of large numbers of newer and older agents under the same conditions have been rare (190–194).

Representative data summarized in Table 20 indicate that most HCAs have very weak effects against the uptake of dopamine and variable effects against the uptake of norepinephrine or serotonin. One fairly consistent finding is that demethylated compounds ("nor-" derivatives or secondary amines, many of which form spontaneously in vivo from tertiary amine HCAs), such as protriptyline, desipramine, nomifensine, and amoxapine, are highly potent against norepinephrine uptake but relatively weak against serotonin uptake, and they are often less sedating than comparable tertiary amine compounds. In addition, N-demethylation of some antipsychotic drugs reduces their sedative-neuroleptic activity and may result in mood-elevating products. A notable example, already mentioned, is amoxapine, which is a selective blocker of norepinephrine uptake, in addition to having some neuroleptic activity (191,196,213).

Of the available antidepressants, trimipramine and doxepin are among the least potent against norepinephrine uptake and should interfere least with the hypotensive actions of postganglionic sympathetic blockers such as guanethidine and be less likely to induce hypertensive interactions with MAO inhibitors. In vivo desmethylation of these antidepressants may alter this suggestion, however, as reported gradual effects of high doses of doxepin against guanethidine (214) seem to illustrate. In addition to in vitro evidence of the blocking of norepinephrine uptake by many HCAs, there is good evidence for similarly potent effects in vivo as evaluated by reduced accumulation of radiolabeled norepinephrine or by diminished depletion of this catecholamine by the adrenergic neurotoxin 6-hydroxydopamine (6-OH-DA), which is taken up by catecholamine-containing nerve terminals— all summarized in Table 22 (194, 195).

Correlations between in vitro and in vivo potencies of antidepressants against norepinephrine uptake are high (r_s = 0.90, Figure 11). On the other hand, a potentially more meaningful relationship between in vivo potency (*not* efficacy) in clinical use and potency against such uptake in vivo or in vitro is weak (r_s = 0.10 to 0.35), as will be discussed further below.

In general, in vivo evidence concerning the blockade of serotonin uptake indicates limited potency of most antidepressants, with the exception of clomipramine and some newer experimental agents such as fluoxetine (Table 22). While several agents that are putatively selective against serotonin uptake are undergoing clinical trials and may have useful antidepressant or antineurotic effects (195), it is *not* proved that their effects are due to facilitation of central serotonergic neurotransmission. Clomipramine and fluoxetine, for example, have some activity against norepinephrine uptake (Table 20). Moreover, paradoxically, at least two agents claimed to have antidepressant effects in European studies

TABLE 22

In Vivo Inhibition of Amine Uptake

Drug	^{3}H-NE (NE)	6-OH-DA (NE)	p-Cl-Amphetamine (5-HT)	Potency Ratios
		ED_{50} (mg/kg)		
Selective against NE				NE:5-HT
Tandamine	—	0.06	>100	1,700
Protriptyline	0.4	0.12	32	120
Desipramine	1.0	0.25	>100	160
Chlorodesipramine	—	1.6	>32	20
Nisoxetine	—	0.9	>100	110
Nortriptyline	—	1.2	>100	83
Imipramine	2.5	3.4	>100	40
Nomifensine	3.0	1.9	—	—
Maprotiline	—	3.9	>100	26
Amitriptyline	4.5	5.3	>100	20
Viloxazine	8.0	5.3	>100	15
Clomipramine	5.5	6.0	10	1.7
Doxepin	14	4.7	>100	11
Selective against 5-HT				5-HT:NE
Fluoxetine	—	>100	0.4	250
Paroxetine	—	28	0.9	31
Norfluoxetine	—	>100	1.6	62
Zimelidine	—	>32	2.8	11
Fluvoxamine	—	>32	15	2.1
Weak against amine uptake				
Mianserin	22	>48	>100	—
Trazodone	>100	>32	>100	—
Iprindole	>100	>100	>100	—

Note: Data are from Clements-Jewery and others (194) and Fuller (195). Tests include block-ade of uptake of ^{3}H-NE by heart, depletion of cardiac NE after administration of 6-hydrox-ydopamine (6-OH-DA), and loss of brain 5-HT after administration of para-chloroamphetam-ine (p-Cl-amphetamine)—all in mouse. The test drug 6-OH-DA is selectively taken up in, and destroys, catecholamine-containing cells; p-Cl-amphetamine is taken up in, and de-pletes, serotonin-containing cells of amine.

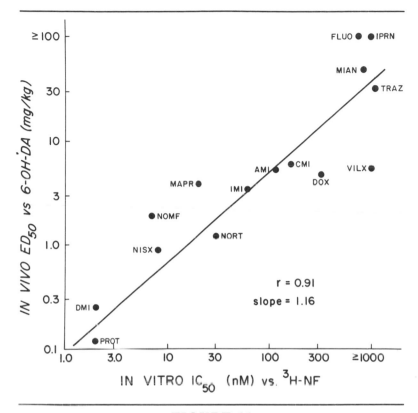

FIGURE 11

Correlation Between in Vitro and in Vivo Inhibition of Uptake into Norepinephrine Nerve Terminals

Note: This analysis is based on data obtained from Tables 18 and 20 for the following 15 chemically dissimilar agents: protriptyline (PRO), desipramine (DMI), nisoxetine (NISX), nomifensine (NOMF), nortriptyline (NORT), maprotiline (MAPR), imipramine (IMI), amitriptyline (AMI), clomipramine (CMI), doxepin (DOX), viloxazine (VILX), trazodone (TRAZ), mianserin (MIAN), fluoxetine (FLUO), and iprindole (IPRN). The log-linear correlation coefficient is $r = +0.91$ (slope = 1.16); the Spearman rank-correlation is $r_s = +0.90$. The data plotted include the half-maximally effective concentration (IC_{50}) of agent that inhibits uptake of labeled norepinephrine (^3H-NE) into synaptosomes from rat brain (Table 20) in vitro versus the half-maximally effective in vivo dose (ED_{50}) that prevents the uptake of the selective catecholamine-depleting neurotoxin, 6-hydroxydopamine (6-OH-DA), from depleting norepinephrine from mouse heart (Table 22).

109

(methysergide and cyproheptadine) are believed to have se-
rotonin-receptor *blocking* actions (215). While facilitation of
serotonin in the brain might be expected to produce sedation or anxiolytic effects, production of true antidepressant
activity by serotonin-facilitating agents, especially in severe
melancholia, requires further critical appraisal.

Most of the new or experimental antidepressants are
pharmacologically similar to older agents, although the
mechanisms of action of a few are obscure (180,185–187).
These atypical antidepressants (see Table 8) are not blockers
of the uptake of monoamines, nor are they MAO inhibitors.
Iprindole and mianserin have recently been suggested to have
subtle influences on the neuronal release of norepinephrine
(195); mianserin also has a weak effect against the uptake of
norepinephrine in vivo, and trazodone may have some serotonin-uptake blocking action at least in vitro (Table 22). These
agents raise serious doubts as to the generality of the mono-
amine-uptake blockade hypothesis of the action of HCAs, as-
suming that the clinical efficacy of these atypical agents is
supported with further experience (71,180,185–188).

While several exceptions to the rule that blockers of
norepinephrine uptake are usually antidepressant can be cited
(amphetamines, cocaine, methylphenidate, mazindol), these
do have short-lasting stimulant actions in humans. On the
other hand, chlorpromazine is also an effective blocker of
norepinephrine uptake (similar in potency to amitriptyline,
clomipramine, or even cocaine—see Table 20). Yet chlorpromazine, a potent dopamine-receptor antagonist, has anti-
agitation effects and is antipsychotic, although its status in
nonpsychotic depressions is obscure (9). The psychomotor
stimulant and agitation-inducing effects of stimulants (or of
other dopamine agonists such as L-DOPA and bromocrip-
tine), which are believed to be mediated by their dopamine-

enhancing actions, limit their usefulness in depression. A sustained versus quick course of action may also help to differentiate stimulants from true antidepressants. Although at least two new antidepressants (nomifensine and bupropion) have some effect against the uptake of dopamine, nomifensine is also an extremely potent blocker of norepinephrine uptake (Tables 20 and 22) and the clinical status and actions of buproprion are still tentative (180). Nomifensine may also act as a stimulant in patients.

Interactions of Antidepressants with Neurotransmitter Receptors

Recent advances have led to many reevaluations of older antidepressants and some experimental antidepressants. These have included studies by biochemical and physiological methods, such as stimulation of the formation of cyclic-AMP or cyclic guanosine monophosphate (cyclic-GMP), behavioral responses to amine agonists, changes in transmitter turnover or firing rates of aminergic neurons, and responses to microapplication of amines to neurons in the CNS. Receptors or binding sites evaluated thus far (Table 23) include traditional α_1 (postsynaptic) and α_2 (partly presynaptic) noradrenergic receptors, β-adrenergic receptors, dopamine (DA) receptors, histamine (H) receptors (types 1 and 2), muscarinic ACh receptors, and serotonin receptors (labeled by 5-HT, type 1; by spiroperidol or ketanserin, in some brain areas, type 2; or by LSD, a mixed and complex interaction) (64,66–69,192,216–222). In addition, the binding of labeled antidepressants themselves has been studied (110,221). Most of the available reports are incomplete or difficult to compare and summarize, but several patterns seem to be emerging.

TABLE 23

Antidepressants versus Amine Receptors: In Vitro Inhibition Constants (nM)

Drug	Typical Clinical Dose (mg/d)	Adrenergic			DA	Muscarinic ACh	Serotonin		Histamine		Anti-depressant
		α_1	α_2	β			$5\text{-}HT_1$	$5\text{-}HT_2$	H_1	H_2	
Protriptyline	30	265	>1,000	3,100	360	115	—	640	48	420	—
Fluoxetine	60	8,000	—	>10,000	6,600	>10,000	10,000	1,300	—	—	—
Mianserin	65	86	35	4,400	2,200	3,900	500	—	3.3	67	100
Nortriptyline	100	71	1,700	15,000	800	950	920	41	17	417	100
Desipramine	100	140	>1,000	4,200	980	2,200	9,500	540	250	317	125
Iprindole	112	9,600	>1,000	21,000	6,300	>10,000	>10,000	1,900	105	200	40,000
Clomipramine	125	55	—	—	—	500	—	—	—	50	8
Amitriptyline	150	24	620	6,800	290	50	1,480	13	0.13	54	20
Imipramine	150	56	>1,000	38,000	610	280	5,000	245	16	153	10
Doxepin	150	23	890	7,100	380	200	720	246	0.4	160	300
Trimipramine	150	45	1,430	—	—	125	42	—	0.1	—	—
Trazodone	300	103	1,500	>10,000	3,000	>50,000	1,700	111	460	>50,000	—
Chlorpromazine	300	4.3	—	>10,000	25	5,700	3,500	15	28	41	300

Note: Data are summarized and averaged (189,192,195,216–221). Note that Spearman rank-correlations (see Table 24) with clinical potency are poor (even excluding neuroleptics).
3H-ligand or test used: α_1: WB-4101; α_2: Clonidine; β: Dihydroxyalprenolol; DA: Spiroperidol, striatum; Muscarinic ACh: Ligand [a] + ileum; $5\text{-}HT_1$: $5\text{-}HT$; $5\text{-}HT_2$: Spiroperidol, cortex; H_1: Mepyramine or cyclic-GMP; H_2: Cyclic-AMP. Antidepressant: Imipramine.

[a] ACh data are averages of data using guinea pig ileum or ³H-quinuclidinyl benzilate (QNB) or other anticholinergic agents as ligands in brain, since results are very similar.

There are few consistent relationships between the in vitro potency of interaction with the above receptors or binding sites and clinical potency (Table 24), even among agents that are similar chemically or similar in some independent pharmacologic characteristic (such as ability to inhibit uptake of norepinephrine; see Tables 18 and 20). One of the few correlations that has limited success in predicting clinical side effects is the apparent anticholinergic activity of antidepressants, as assayed by competition with a potent muscarinic antagonist such as ^{3}H-quinuclidinyl benzilate (^{3}H-QNB) or in the stimulation of cyclic-GMP synthesis by neural tissues (65,67,216–219).

These studies reveal that, among traditional antidepressants, amitriptyline is most potent, followed closely by protriptyline, doxepin, and imipramine, while the desmethylated products desipramine and nortriptyline are much less potent in vitro and somewhat less anticholinergic in man (although less strikingly so than is sometimes supposed). Moreover, some new agents, such as iprindole, fluoxetine, trazodone, alprazolam, and mianserin, are virtually without anticholinergic activity (Table 23). Since the correlation between anticholinergic activity and clinical potency generally is rather weak (Table 24), an antimuscarinic hypothesis of antidepressant action is not supported. Nevertheless, since there is a rough correspondence between these anticholinergic actions and ability to induce atropine-like poisoning in patients, and to some degree cardiac toxicity, screening of new agents in this way may lead to less toxic medications.

Other short-term receptor interactions have been much less helpful in suggesting a hypothesis of drug action or a generally useful principle to guide drug development. There is some tendency for strong anti-α_1 interactions to correlate roughly with hypotensive or sedative actions, notably of doxepin and amitriptyline (as well as chlorpromazine), which are the most potent (Table 22). Interactions with α_2 receptors are generally very weak, with the notable exception of mianserin, leading to the hypothesis that this agent may facilitate the release of norepinephrine from nerve terminals by blocking presynaptic α_2 receptors that are believed to throttle the release of norepinephrine (195).

TABLE 24

Correlations Among Clinical Potency and Actions of Antidepressants

Factors (Potencies)	r	Number of Agents	P
Adrenergic			
In vitro vs. in vivo NE uptake	14	+0.89	<0.001
Clinical vs. in vitro NE uptake			
All available agents	19	+0.31	NS
Imipramine analogs only			
(r_s)	7	+0.81	<0.05
(r_{xy})	7	+0.63	~0.05
Clinical vs. in vivo NE uptake	16	+0.10	NS
Clinical vs NE:5-HT anti-uptake ratio	19	−0.06	NS
NE uptake vs. α_1 receptor blockade	10	+0.32	NS
Clinical vs. anti-α_1 receptor	10	−0.73	<0.02
Clinical vs. anti-NE uptake:anti-α_1 ratio	10	+0.65	<0.04
Clinical vs. anti-DA receptor	10	−0.20	NS
Serotonergic			
Clinical vs. 5-HT uptake in vitro	19	+0.15	NS
Anti-5-HT$_1$ vs. 5-HT$_2$ receptors	7	+0.88	<0.02
Clinical vs. anti-5-HT$_1$	8	−0.10	NS
Clinical vs. anti-5-HT$_2$	6	−0.31	NS

TABLE 24 (continued)

Correlations Among Clinical Potency and Actions of Antidepressants

Factors (Potencies)	r	Number of Agents	P
Histaminergic and muscarinic			
Anti-H_1 vs. H_2 receptors	9	$+0.49$	NS
Clinical vs. H_1	8	-0.41	NS
Clinical vs. H_2	9	-0.51	NS
Clinical vs. ACh (muscarinic)	11	-0.10	NS

Note: Data are from Tables 18, 20, and 23; clinical potency (*not* efficacy) data are from Paykel (223) and Baldessarini (8). Correlations are by nonparametric rank method (Spearman, r_s) for N agents; an evaluation of linear regression (r_{xy}) of clinical potency versus anti NE uptake for imipramine analogs reveals a suggestive correlation ($r_{xy} = +0.63$ of low power, as slope -0.24). Anti-β activity (in vitro) is too weak to justify analysis.

The general impressions given by the above are that (a) lower potency correlates with more anti-ACh, anti-H_1, and anti-α_1 effect (and possibly greater risk of sedative and cardiovascular side effects); (b) antidepressant effect tends to correlate with greater anti-NE uptake effect (but this may be an artifact of drug development procedures) and less anti-α_1 effect; (c) most agents are weak β blockers (may *permit* β down-regulation); (d) there is little effect on DA uptake or receptors; (e) none of these effects, alone, seems to account for antidepressant effects.

If potentiation of action of norepinephrine is an important effect of many antidepressants, that effect is especially likely to be mediated by postsynaptic α_1 receptors. This hypothesis is suggested by the correlational analyses summarized in Table 24. Thus, although the potency against norepinephrine uptake (in vitro or in vivo) correlates only weakly with clinical potency (*not* efficacy) of heterocyclic antidepressants, there is a significant *inverse* correlation of clinical potency ($r_s = 0.73$) with α_1-blocking potency. Moreover, clinical potency correlates significantly with the ratio of potencies of

115

blocking norepinephrine uptake to blocking α_1 receptors ($r_s = +0.65$), although the effects on uptake and α_1 sites themselves are not significantly intercorrelated ($r_s = +0.32$).

These relationships thus suggest that increased availability of norepinephrine (by potent uptake blockade) along with *weak* α_1 blockade may be desirable characteristics in an antidepressant. The β-receptor desensitizing action of repeated antidepressant treatment (discussed below) provides further support for this hypothesis. While this approach of correlating in vivo potencies with antidepressant potencies in test systems (Table 24) is of much more limited power and generality than, say, the correlation of neuroleptic potency with antagonism of ^{3}H-butyrophenone binding (224,225), it does yield some interesting relationships.

Interactions between antidepressants and dopamine receptors are generally weak. The relatively sedative agents doxepin and amitriptyline and the 7-OH metabolite of amoxapine (rare in humans), but also the nonsedating agent protriptyline, have moderate potency in one or both of two test systems (binding of ^{3}H-spiroperidol or formation of cyclic-AMP in tissue of basal ganglia) (see Table 23) (191,216). Similarly, several of these agents are relatively potent histamine (especially H_1) receptor antagonists—particularly doxepin, one of the most potent antihistamines known, although there is only weak potency-order correspondence with either H_1 or H_2 interactions and clinical potency, at least for the rather small number of agents so tested (Tables 23 and 24).

LONG-TERM EFFECTS OF ANTIDEPRESSANTS

Changes in the characteristics of amine receptors following one to three weeks of antidepressant treatment are more promising than immediate interactions in providing clues to the actions of antidepressants that may underlie clinical effects. Notably, there is growing support for the impression that presynaptic (α_2) noradrenergic receptors may become less sensitive (or abundant) after repeated treatment with an antidepressant. This change may lead to *increased* release of norepinephrine per nerve impulse in cardiac or brain tissue, as well as to decreased responsiveness to exogenous α_2 (presumably presynaptic) but not α_1 (postsynaptic) agonists (107,108,226). This change appears to be correlated with a rise in norepinephrine turnover and in the firing rates of noradrenergic neurons in the locus ceruleus of the brainstem (226), although basal levels of plasma MHPG may actually be decreased in patients (108). These effects have been evaluated best with desipramine.

Amitriptyline and other antidepressants have also been reported recently to lead to increased response of α_1 receptors (227,228) or binding of α_1 and muscarinic agents to receptors in brain tissue (229), although others do not agree (230). The duration, functional significance, and generality of these effects among chemically dissimilar antidepressants require further study.

It has also been noted for several years that repeated administration of antidepressants of several chemical types (including MAO inhibitors and some atypical newer agents such as iprindole, which lacks acute effects on the metabolism or actions of norepinephrine) led to *diminished* sensitivity of β-adrenergic responses in brain tissue. (This is also true of ECT but not of treatment with other classes of neuropharmaceuticals.) This change has been well evaluated with norepinephrine- or isoproterenol-sensitive formation of cyclic-AMP by cerebral tissues, as well as with receptor-binding methods (notably, with tritium-labeled β antagonists such as dihydroalprenolol) (70,193,216,230–233).

While such a "down-regulation" of sensitivity to norepinephrine (typically by 20–30%) seems counterintuitive in view of traditional hypotheses concerning adrenergic insufficiency in depression, the physiologic significance of such a change is uncertain. There is some evidence that norepinephrine microiontophoretically applied to β-sensitive CNS neurons may also be less effective (234,235). Such changes are likely to represent one of several mechanisms that tend to restore homeostasis of central neurotransmission, rather than to represent a true net loss of noradrenergic neurotransmission, the postsynaptic effects of which are complex, remote, and poorly understood neurophysiologically (236).

Almost certainly β blockade per se is *not* an adequate explanation for antidepressant effects; indeed, the β antagonist propranolol is even suspected of inducing depression in some patients (237). Moreover, chlorpromazine and amphetamine, which are not considered antidepressants, can exert effects like those of imipramine on β receptors (Table 25). Regardless of the functional significance of such a short-lived and reversible change in β-adrenergic sensitivity, the generality of the effect across many classes of agents is striking and might lead to new methods for predicting antidepressant activity of new substances. A summary of findings based on receptor binding or assays of the stimulation of cyclic-AMP synthesis is provided in Table 25 (193,216,217,230–232,238–245).

While there are few reports of consistent long-term changes in the binding of labeled ligands to α_1, acetylcholine, histamine, or dopamine receptors (216,229,230) following treatment with an antidepressant, some interesting findings in serotonin systems are emerging. For the binding of ^{3}H-serotonin itself (5-HT$_1$ receptors), there have been reports of variable and somewhat inconsistent decreases in binding-site density (Table 25). Similar antidepressant treatments may produce sustained increases in the levels of serotonin in brain, notably with inhibitors of MAO type A (238), but less consistently with HCAs (230,246). More intriguing, however, are data indicating a fall (of 20–40%) in binding of ^{3}H-spiroperidol, which is believed to bind to a class of serotonin receptors in cerebral cortex designated type 2 (in contrast to selective labeling of dopamine D-2 sites in the basal ganglia with this ligand (Table 24) (216). Curiously, these chemical observations seem to contradict results of behavioral and neurophysiological studies (228,247–250), which consistently indicate an increased sensitivity to serotonin in several brain regions after repeated treatment (weeks) with typical and even some atypical antidepressants, such as iprindole.

In the dopamine system, there is still no evidence of altered receptor binding sites or of postsynaptic changes in sensitivity to this catecholamine (216,230). Nevertheless, there have been intriguing recent reports of behavioral (239) and neurophysiologic (241,242) changes consistent with a *decrease* in sensitivity of putative presynaptic dopamine receptors that are believed to throttle the production and release of dopamine. In addition, ECT may alter presynaptic (242) as well as postsynaptic (244) receptors so as to enhance dopamine neurotransmission, perhaps especially in the mesolimbic dopamine system (244). There is also some indirect behavioral evidence of increased release of dopamine in the rat by limbic intracranial self-stimulation after repeated treatment with desipramine (251). These effects may thus *in-*

TABLE 25

Diminution of Receptor Binding in Cerebral Cortex After Antidepressant Treatment

Treatment	Norepinephrine		Serotonin			Dopamine	
	Beta Adrenergic Cyclase	Binding	Binding 5-HT$_1$	5-HT$_2$	Iontophoretic Actions	Postsynaptic Binding	Presynaptic Stimulation
ECT	+	+	?	?	+	0	+
Amitriptyline	+	+	0	+	+	0	+
Imipramine	+	+	+	+	+	0	+
Clomipramine	+	+	?	?	+	0	?
Doxepin	?	+	?	?	?	?	?
Nortriptyline	?	+	?	?	?	?	?
Desipramine	+	+	+/0	+	+	0	?
Nisoxetine	+	0	?	?	?	?	?
Iprindole	+/0	+/0	0	+	+	0	+
Trazodone	?	+/0	?	+	?	?	?
Buproprion	?	+	?	+	?	?	?
Mianserin	+/0	+/0	?	+	?	?	+
Methysergide	?	0	?	0	?	?	?

120

Drug							
Fluoxetine	+	0	0	0	?	?	?
Zimelidine	+	?	?	?	0	?	?
Phenelzine	?	+	?	?	?	?	?
Nialamide	+	+	+	?	?	?	?
Pargyline	+	+/0	+/0	+	?	0	?
Tranylcypromine	+	+	?	+	?	?	?
Clorgyline	?	+	+	?	0	?	?
Deprenyl	?	0	0	?	?	?	?
d-Amphetamine	+	+	?	?	?	?	+
Cocaine	?	0	?	?	?	?	?
Chlorpromazine	+	0	0	0	?	?	?
Haloperidol	0	0	0	0	?	?	?
Diazepam	0	0	?	?	?	?	?
Lithium	?	0	+	?	?	?	?

Note: Binding sites (³H-labeling agent) *without* consistent changes include: 5-HT$_1$ (unless inhibitors of MAO-A were given), α_1 (WB-4101) with few agents tested, H$_1$ (mepyramine), DA (spiroperidol in striatum), muscarinic ACh (QNB); 5-HT$_2$ (defined by spiroperidol in cortex); LSD binding (5-HT$_{1,2}$) also decreases; α_2 may also diminish, based on indirect evidence (mostly desipramine). The effect on β receptors disappears within a week after stopping desipramine. There are no effects after single doses. Rats were typically treated for 2–3 weeks with large doses of drugs and tissue was taken one day after the end of treatment. Based on data from 15 studies (193, 216, 227, 222, 230–232, 238–245). Experimental conditions included: stimulation of cyclic-AMP formation in cerebral cortex slices by NE or isoproterenol; binding with ³H-dihydroalprenolol (β), ³H-5-HT (5-HT$_1$), ³H-spiroperidol (5-HT$_2$ in cortex; DA in striatum); or behavioral or neurophysiologic evidence of decreased responsiveness of DA cells to low "presynaptic" doses of the direct DA agonist, apomorphine. Symbols represent: + = effect reported, 0 = effect not found, ? = effect not evaluated.

crease the functional availability to, or effects of dopamine at, postsynaptic dopamine receptors and may contribute to the mood- and behavior-activating effects of antidepressant treatments. The effects may evolve over time even if the treatment itself is not given repeatedly every day (241,242), although this intriguing phenomenon has never been described in a clinical setting.

Despite these interesting leads, current knowledge of the physiologic relations between membrane binding changes and regulation of neurotransmitter function is too incomplete to permit a coherent interpretation of these complex and sometimes seemingly paradoxical findings. Yet their fair consistency across classes of antidepressant treatments (including some atypical agents and ECT) is quite compelling (Table 25). This approach therefore deserves further attention as a contribution to understanding the actions of antidepressant treatments or to the development of more powerful predictive tests to aid in the development of new treatments, especially as a complement to behavioral investigations in the search for new antidepressants (252).

The application of tritium-labeled antidepressants themselves in search of unique tissue binding sites or receptors has not led to important insights, to date, concerning antidepressant actions, although they may permit development of sensitive radioreceptor assays for antidepressant drugs. A major problem has been that potencies of interaction of drugs in such binding assays, to the extent that they have been studied, correlate poorly with clinical potency (Table 24). This result may reflect the complex interactions of such labeled compounds with tissue, including cholinergic, serotonergic, and histaminergic receptors and (especially) serotonin transport sites or other sites on serotonin cells (110,217,

221,253,254), as well as norepinephrine uptake sites (255).

CONCLUSIONS CONCERNING THE PHARMACOLOGY OF ANTIDEPRESSANTS

Clearly, this is one of the most exciting times in the development and evaluation of antidepressants since the introduction of modern antidepressants in the 1950s and 1960s and the work leading to amine hypotheses of their actions in the 1960s. There is now an unprecedented array of new agents and of new techniques and ideas concerning drug actions.

Still, there are limitations and remaining problems, both theoretical and practical (Table 26). We are faced with an apparently still irreducible residue of 20–30% of patients who respond poorly or not at all to any of the available or experimental treatments for depression (9, 200–202). Newer agents at least promise alternatives for some patients and, very importantly, additional safety. Needed is a more coherent theory to predict antidepressant activity and so aid the development or discovery of more nearly ideal antidepressants. Also needed are more consistently effective agents for use in severe as well as mild depression—agents that are less toxic in therapeutic doses, especially in the elderly, and not lethal in suicidal or accidental overdoses and that are less likely to interact unfavorably with other medicinal agents.

There are also additional problems, related to antidepressant and other medical treatments of major mood disorders, that bear on research directed at a better understanding of the disorders themselves (Table 26). These include an ethical dilemma: Is it justifiable to withhold the use of reasonably effective and safe, if imperfect, treatments in the conduct of a therapeutic experiment, in order to have a placebo or no-treatment group? It is also highly probable that the use of existing treatments has introduced, and will continue to introduce, artifacts into biological measurements in patients who have severe mood disorders, even if brief drug "wash-out" periods are included.

Yet another problem that is still not widely appreciated is that clinical presentation of mood disorders is modified by treatment at several levels. "Classic" cases are less often

TABLE 26

Problems for Research on Depression and Antidepressants

Topic	Problem
Antidepressants	Efficacy: 20–30% of cases respond poorly
	Toxicity: newer agents seem less toxic to heart and CNS, but efficacy is not always well supported
	Pharmacokinetics: generalizations about "therapeutic levels" are uncertain
	Pharmacodynamics: lack of coherent theory or method to predict new agents, short of clinical trials, vs. more "me-too" drugs
Depression	Treatment can modify clinical presentations (e.g., mania as psychosis without excitement; depression with loss of vegetative symptoms)
	Partial success of available treatments discourages inclusion of a placebo group in therapeutic experiments and raises an ethical dilemma
	Recent treatment can induce artifacts in biologic measurements, even after a nominal drug "wash-out" period (typically only a few days)

available at research centers, since they are now increasingly successfully treated close to home. Cases that are evaluated during or after treatment are often very different from untreated cases (for example, probable mania may appear to be an acute psychosis without obvious excitement if a lithium salt is being used; a case of melancholia may be partly modified by prior treatment with an antidepressant so as to minimize many of the vegetative symptoms).

The present overview suggests several tentative conclusions. It is almost certain that no single biochemical or neurophysiological hypothesis accounts for the actions of all antidepressants. While many have actions that block norepinephrine uptake, these may reflect some circularity of reasoning and of the process of pharmaceutical development. In fact, correlations between anti-uptake potency and clinical potency are rather weak (Table 24), although the range of clinical potencies is limited, and it may be inappropriate to make comparisons across chemical classes of agents. Receptor binding analyses suggest that antihistamine effects (especially at H_1 receptors) are most striking in some agents of relatively low clinical potency that may also be relatively sedative antidepressants (Table 23). Anticholinergic effects (at muscarinic receptors) may help to predict toxic in vivo actions. It is hypothesized that the combination of high potency against norepinephrine uptake, low potency against α_1 blockade, and a tendency to down-regulate β-adrenergic receptors may be especially characteristic of antidepressants that have relatively low sedative and hypotensive actions. A major theoretical limitation to addressing the question of how antidepressants work is our limited understanding of the pathophysiology of depressive illness and the growing impression that both depressions and antidepressants are biologically heterogeneous.

4

Summary and Conclusions

Mood disorders are among the most common major psychiatric disorders; the risk rates are about 12%. The theory and management of severe depression and manic-depressive illnesses have virtually been revolutionized by the developments in psychopharmacology since 1950. Effective short-term and preventive treatment of depression is afforded by tricyclic, MAO-inhibitor, atypical, and experimental heterocyclic antidepressants; neuroleptic agents are clearly effective in mania; and lithium salts aid long-term management of manic-depressive illness. Knowledge of the actions of these agents is increasingly rich and complex. Much of the current interest is on altered sensitivity of amine receptors, since such later effects are typically different from immediate actions, and so tend to parallel the time course of clinical antidepressant actions.

Biomedical theories concerning the pathophysiology of depression have in the past been dominated by partial understanding of drug actions. The resulting inductive approach to formulating and testing of hypotheses has enriched psychiatric research and supported progress in pharmacology. Nevertheless, clinical searches for direct metabolic support for amine hypotheses of mood disorders have been inconclusive. Recent moves beyond the testing of amine hypotheses are enriching the clinical, descriptive, diagnostic, genetic, endocrinologic, and neurophysiologic understanding of the syndromes of depression. These approaches have led to compelling support for the division of major mood disorders into bipolar and nonbipolar (unipolar) subtypes, to diagnostic laboratory tests that promise clinical utility comparable to that of tests in general medicine, and to unprecedented enlightenment in the clinical management of manic and depressed patients. These developments represent the most substantial contributions of a biomedical approach to psychiatry to date and support the clinical and scientific value of the approach.

There have been important recent advances in the development of new antidepressant agents and in understanding the actions of those available since the 1950s; see Table 27. Five new heterocyclic antidepressants have been introduced into American medicine in 1979 (trimipramine), 1980 (amoxapine and maprotiline), and 1981–82 (alprazolam and trazodone), and there are more than 70 additional experimental antidepressants in clinical use or under study abroad. Most of the newer drugs are remarkably similar pharmacologically to imipramine and older agents, especially in their interactions with the uptake of norepinephrine. A few experimental agents selectively potentiate serotonin, and still other atypical agents (such as iprindole, mianserin, trazodone, and perhaps alprazolam) have little effect on aminergic neurotransmitter systems and lack certain undesirable side effects, such as anticholinergic actions and cardiac depressant effects. Some of the newer and more atypical agents require further clinical evaluation in severely depressed or melancholic patients; they have been best evaluated in neurotic

TABLE 27

Growing Clinical Indications for Antidepressants

Heterocyclics	MAO Inhibitors
Acute major depression	Acute major depression (high doses)
Prevent unipolar relapses	Maintenance use less well established
Panic disorder	Panic disorder (preferred ?)
Hysteroid or "borderline" dysphorias [a]	Hysteroid dysphoria
Other secondary depressions in psychiatric or neurological disorders [a]	Other secondary depressions [a]
Obsessive compulsive disorder (especially clomipramine) [a]	Post-traumatic neurosis [a]
Paranoid disorders (acute) [a]	
Chronic pain [a]	
Peripheral diabetic neuropathy [a]	
Migraine [a]	
Narcolepsy (especially clomipramine) [a]	
Sleep apnea (especially protriptyline) [a]	
Anorexia nervosa and bulimia [a]	
School phobia	
Hyperactivity disorder [a]	
Enuresis [a]	
Peptic ulcer (especially amitriptyline) [a]	

[a]These indications remain experimental, controversial, and incompletely established (202).

129

SUMMARY AND CONCLUSIONS

outpatients who have anxiety and somatic symptoms, as well as mild or moderately severe depression.

The partial success of available antidepressants has led to difficulties in the conduct of appropriate placebo-controlled trials in severely ill patients, and most recent therapeutic trials compare a new agent with an established antidepressant. Recent studies of actions of antidepressants have concentrated on interactions with neurotransmitter receptors and have included increasing numbers of prolonged studies

TABLE 28

Predictors of Favorable Response to Antidepressants

Status	Predictor
Well established	Endogenomorphic, vital, melancholic depression, acute
	Past success of biologic treatment
	Dose above equivalent of 125 mg/day of imipramine
	Blood-drug levels above 100 ng/ml for most heterocyclic agents
	Platelet MAO inhibited by more than 85% (phenelzine)
Investigational suggestion	Activation of behavior by 20–30 mg of amphetamine in an acute test dose
	Relatively *low* urinary MHPG in *high* CSF 5-HIAA levels may predict preferential response to imipramine, desipramine, or maprotiline; the opposite in response to amitriptyline or clomipramine

Note: Based on information reviewed in the text and by Bielski and Friedel (256).

130

of drug effects in animals, leading to provocative findings suggestive of altered sensitivity of adrenergic and serotonin receptors in brain.

There is, as yet, no compelling general theory of the mechanism of antidepressant action, in part due to the lack of a compelling neurobiological or metabolic theory of depression itself. Moreover, available methods of screening potential new antidepressants have been heavily biased by attention to potentiation of norepinephrine as a model of antidepressant drug action.

Modern biochemical approaches, combined with improved methods of diagnosis and clinical evaluation of depressed patients, has led to better methods of matching patients and treatments and in predicting short- and long-term outcome; see Table 28. Much more information is needed regarding the long-term, or so-called "prophylactic," use of antidepressants and other mood-stabilizing agents, such as lithium salts or carbamazepine (Tegretol). While at least six relatively short-term follow-up studies indicate that heterocyclic antidepressants probably have a preventive effect in recurrent depression ($53 \pm 10\%$ rate of relapse on placebo versus $19 \pm 8\%$ on drug, overall), little is known about optimal choice of drug or dose, or about safety or efficacy after several years of such treatment (8,202,257–259).

On the basis of the material reviewed in this monograph, and given the limitations of currently available drugs, some suggestions have been made in Table 27 as to the increasing range of diagnostic groups in which benefits from a heterocyclic or MAO-inhibitor antidepressant might be expected (8,180,202) and in Table 28 as to means of obtaining optimal results in treating depression.

131

REFERENCES

1. Diagnostic and Statistical Manual, 3rd ed. American Psychiatric Association, Washington, DC, 1980, 494 pp.
2. Boyd JH, Weissman MM: Epidemiology of affective disorders: A re-examination and future directions. Arch Gen Psychiatry 38:1039–1046, 1981.
3. Silverman G: The Epidemiology of Depression. Johns Hopkins Press, Baltimore, 1968.
4. Winokur G, Clayton P, Reich T: Manic-Depressive Disease. Mosby Co., St. Louis, 1970.
5. Slater E, Cowie V: The Genetics of Mental Disorders. Oxford University Press, London, 1971.
6. Hollister LE: Tricyclic antidepressants. New Engl J Med 299:1106–1109; 1168–1172, 1978.
7. Baldessarini RJ: Mood Drugs. Disease-A-Month 11:1–65, 1977.
8. Baldessarini RJ: Chemotherapy in Psychiatry. Harvard University Press, Cambridge, 1977 (2nd ed, in press, 1983).
9. Baldessarini RJ: Drugs and the treatment of psychiatric disorders, in The Pharmacological Basis of Therapeutics, 6th ed. Edited by Gilman AG, Goodman LS, Gilman A. MacMillan Co., New York, 1980, pp 391–447.

10. Fink M: Convulsive Therapy: Theory and Practice. Raven Press, New York, 1979.
11. Kraepelin E: Manic-Depressive Insanity and Paranoia. Edited by Barklay M, Robertson GM. E&S Livingston, Edinburgh, 1921.
12. Leonhard K, Korff I, Schulz H: Die temperamente in den familien der monopolaren and bipolaren phasischen psychosen. Psychiatrie Neurol 143:416–434, 1962.
13. Pope HG Jr, Lipinski JF, Cohen BM, Axelrod DT: "Schizoaffective disorder": An invalid diagnosis? A comparison of schizoaffective disorder, schizophrenia, and affective disorder. Am J Psychiatry 137:921–927, 1980.
14. Taylor MA, Abrams R, Hayman MA: The classification of affective disorders—A reassessment of the bipolar-unipolar dichotomy: A clinical, laboratory, and family study. J Affect Disorders 2:95–109, 1980.
15. Fieve RR, Kumbaraci T, Dunner DL: Lithium prophylaxis of depression in bipolar I, bipolar II, and unipolar patients. Am J Psychiatry 133:925–929, 1976.
16. Dunner DL, Fleiss, JL, Fieve RR: The course of development of mania in patients with recurrent depression. Am J Psychiatry 133:905–908, 1976.
17. Bunney WE Jr, Goodwin FK, Murphy DL: The "switch process" in manic-depressive illness. Arch Gen Psychiatry 27:295–317, 1972.
18. Lewis JL, Winokur G: The induction of mania: A natural history study with controls. Arch Gen Psychiatry 39:303–306, 1982.
19. Grof P: Personal communication, October 1981.
20. Grof P, Lane J, MacCrimmon D, et al: Clinical and laboratory correlates of the response to long-term lithium treatment, in Origin, Intervention, and Treatment of Af-

fective Disorders. Edited by Strömgren E, Schou M. Academic Press, New York, 1979, pp 28–40.

21. Arana GW, Akiskal H, Baldessarini RJ, Barreira P: Paranoid illnesses responsive to antidepressants (submitted for publication, 1982).

22. Finklestein S, Benowitz LI, Baldessarini RJ, et al: Mood, vegetative signs, and dexamethasone suppression test after stroke. Ann Neurol (in press, 1982).

23. Hyman S, Cohen BJ, Pope GH Jr, Lipinski JF: What does a research diagnosis of schizophrenia mean? (unpublished manuscript, 1982).

24. Gershon ES: The search for genetic markers in affective disorders, in Psychopharmacology: A Generation of Progress. Edited by Lipton MA, DiMascio A, Killam KF. Raven Press, New York, 1978, pp 1197–1212.

25. Perris C: Genetic transmission of depressive psychosis. Acta Psychiat Neurol Scand (Suppl. 203):45–52, 1968.

26. Price JS: The genetics of depressive behavior, in Recent Developments in Affective Disorders. Edited by Coppen A, Walk A. Br J Psychiatry (special publication No. 2):37–54, 1968.

27. Von Trostorff S: Über die hereditäre belastung bei den bipolaren und monopolaren phasischen psychosen. Schweiz Arch Neurol Neurochir Psychiatrie 102:235–240, 1968.

28. Zerbin-Rüdin E: Zur genetik der depressiven erkrankungen, in Das Depressive Syndrom. Edited by Hippius H, Selbach H. Urban & Schwarzenberg, Munich, 1969, pp 37–56.

29. Cadoret RJ, Winokur G, Clayton P: Family history studies, VII: Manic-depressive disease versus depressive disease. Br J Psychiatry 116:625–635, 1970.

30. Winokur G, Cadoret RJ, Dorzab J, et al: Depressive disease: A genetic study. Arch Gen Psychiatry 24:135–144, 1971.
31. Cadoret R, Winokur G: Genetic studies of affective disorders, in The Nature and Treatment of Depression. Edited by Flach FF, Draghi SC. John Wiley & Sons, New York, 1975, pp 335–346.
32. Tsuang MT: Genetics of affective disorder, in The Psychobiology of Depression. Edited by Mendels J. Spectrum Publications, New York, 1975, pp 85–100.
33. Allen MG: Twin studies of affective illness. Arch Gen Psychiatry 33:1476–1478, 1976.
34. Gershon ES, Bunney WE Jr, Lechman JF, et al: The inheritance of affective disorders: A review of data and hypotheses. Behav Genetics 6:227–261, 1976.
35. Mendelwicz J: Application of genetic techniques to psychiatric research, in Biological Bases of Psychiatric Disorders. Edited by Frazer A, Winokur A. Spectrum Publications, New York, 1977, pp 79–88.
36. Winokur G: Mania and depression: Family studies and genetics in relation to treatment, in Psychopharmacology: A Generation of Progress. Edited by Lipton, MA, DiMascio A, Killam KF. Raven Press, New York, 1978, pp 1213–1221.
37. Winokur G, Tsuang MT, Crowe RR: The Iowa 500: Affective disorder in relatives of manic and depressed patients. Am J. Psychiatry 139:209–212, 1982.
38. Dunner DL, Go RCP, Fieve RR: A family study of patients with bipolar II illness (bipolar depression with hypomania). Presented at the annual meeting of the American College of Neuropsychopharmacology, San Juan, PR, December 1980.
39. Egeland JA: Affective disorders among the Amish: 1976–

1980. Presented at the annual meeting of the American College of Neuropsychopharmacology, San Juan, PR, December 1980.

40. Taylor MA, Abrams R: Early- and late-onset bipolar illness. Arch Gen Psychiatry 38:58–61, 1981.

41. Hirschfeld RMA, Cross CK: Epidemiology of affective disorders: Psychosocial risk factors. Arch Gen Psychiatry 39:35–46, 1982.

42. Grof P, Angst J, Haines T: The clinical course of depression, in Classification and Prediction of Outcome of Depression (Hoechst Symposia Medica, Vol. 8). Schattauer Verlag, New York, 1974, pp 141–148.

43. Zis A, Grof P, Webster M, et al: Prediction of relapse in recurrent affective disorders. Psychopharmacol Bull 16:47–49, 1980.

44 Mendelwicz J, Rainer JD: Adoption study supporting genetic transmission of manic-depressive illness. Nature 268:327–329, 1977.

45. Cadoret RJ: Evidence for genetic inheritance of primary affective disorder in adoptees. Am J Psychiatry 135:463–466, 1978.

46. Kety SS, Rosenthal D, Wender PH, et al: Unpublished observations cited at a McLean Hospital seminar, 1980.

47. Everett GM, Tolman JEP: Mode of action of rauwolfia alkaloids and motor activity, in Biological Psychiatry. Edited by Masserman J. Grune & Stratton, New York, 1959, pp 75–81.

48. Jacobsen E: The theoretical basis of the chemotherapy of depression, in Depression: Proceedings of a Symposium at Cambridge, September 1959. Edited by Davies EB. Cambridge University Press, New York, 1964, p 208.

49. Weil-Malherbe H: The biochemistry of the functional psychoses. Adv Enzymol 29:479–553, 1967.

50. Schildkraut JJ: Neuropsychopharmacology and the Affective Disorders. Little, Brown & Co., Boston, 1970.

51. Van Praag, HM: Amine hypotheses of affective disorders, in Handbook of Psychopharmacology, Vol. 13. Edited by Iversen LL, Iversen SD, Snyder SH. Plenum Press, New York, 1978, pp 187–297.

52. Janowski DS, El-Yousef MK, Davis JM: Acetylcholine and depression. Psychosom Med 36:248–257, 1974.

53. Sjöström R, Roos B-E: 5-Hydroxyindoleacetic acid and homovanillic acid in cerebrospinal fluid in manic-depressive psychosis. Eur J Clin Pharmacol 4:170–176, 1972.

54. Andén N-E, Dahlström A, Fuxe K, et al: Ascending neurons to the telencephalon and diencephalon. Acta Physiol Scand 67:313–326, 1966.

55. Baldessarini RJ, Karobath M: Biochemical physiology of central synapses. Ann Rev Physiol 35:273–304, 1973.

56. Baldessarini RJ: Biogenic amine hypotheses in affective disorders, in The Nature and Treatment of Depression. Edited by Flach FF, Draghi S. Plenum Press, New York, 1975, pp. 347–385.

57. Cooper JR, Bloom FE, Roth RH: The Biochemical Basis of Neuropharmacology, 3rd ed. Oxford University Press, New York, 1979.

58. Glowinski J, Baldessarini RJ: Metabolism of norepinephrine in the central nervous system. Pharmacol Rev 18:1201–1238, 1966.

59. Bunney WE Jr, Garland BL: Selected aspects of amine and receptor hypotheses of affective illness. J Clin Psychopharmacol 1:3S–11S, 1981.

60. Goodwin FK, Ebert MH, Bunney WE Jr: Mental effects of reserpine in man, in Psychiatric Complications of

Medical Drugs. Edited by Shader R. Raven Press, New York, 1972, pp 73–101.

61. Meltzer HY, Stahl SM: The dopamine hypothesis of schizophrenia: A review. Schizophrenia Bull 2:19–76, 1976.

62. Schildkraut JJ, Roffman M, Orsulak PJ, et al: Effects of short- and long-term administration of tricyclic antidepressants and lithium on norepinephrine turnover in brain. Pharmacopsychiatry 9:193–202, 1976.

63. Svenssen TH, Usdin T: Feedback inhibition of brain noradrenaline neurons by tricyclic antidepressants: α-Receptor mediation. Science 202:1089–1091, 1978.

64. Fuxe K, Ögren S-O, Agnati L, et al: On the mechanism of action of the antidepressant drugs amitriptyline and nortriptyline: Evidence for 5-hydroxytryptamine receptor blocking activity. Neurosci Letters 6:339–343, 1977.

65. Snyder SII, Yamamura H: Antidepressants and the muscarinic acetylcholine receptor. Arch Gen Psychiatry 34:236–239, 1977.

66. U'Prichard DC, Greenberg DA, Sheehan PP, et al: Tricyclic antidepressants: Therapeutic properties and affinity for α-noradrenergic receptor binding sites in the brain. Science 199:197–198, 1978.

67. Richelson E: Tricyclic antidepressants and histamine H_1 receptors. Mayo Clin Proc 54:669–674, 1979.

68. Crews FT, Smith CB: Presynaptic alpha receptor subsensitivity after long-term antidepressant treatment. Science 202:322–324, 1978.

69. Wang RY, Aghajanian GK: Enhanced sensitivity of amygdaloid neurons to serotonin and norepinephrine after chronic antidepressant treatment. Comm Psychopharmacol 4:83–90, 1980.

70. Vetulani J, Stawarz RJ, Dingell JV, et al: A possible

common mechanism of action of antidepressent treatments. Naunyn-Schmiedeberg's Arch Pharmacol 293:109–114, 1976.

71. Pinder RM: Antidepressants. Ann Reports Med Chem 15:1–11, 1980.

72. Zis AP, Goodwin FK: Novel antidepressants and the biogenic amine hypothesis of depression. Arch Gen Psychiatry 36:1097–1107, 1979.

73. Carroll BJ: Monoamine precursors in the treatment of depression. Clin Pharmacol Ther 12:743–761, 1971.

74. Baldessarini RJ: The basis for amine hypotheses in affective disorders: A critical evaluation. Arch Gen Psychiatry 32:1087–1093, 1975.

75. Murphy DL, Campbell IC, Costa JL: The brain serotonergic system in the affective disorders, in Prog Neuropsychopharmacology 2:5–31, 1978. Vol. 2. Pergamon Press, Oxford, 1978.

76. Schildkraut JJ: Current status of the catecholamine hypothesis of affective disorders, in Psychopharmacology: A Generation of Progress. Edited by Lipton MA, DiMascio A, Killam KF. Raven Press, New York, 1978, pp 1223–1234.

77. Garver DL, Davis JM: Biogenic amine hypotheses of affective disorders. Life Sciences 24:383–394, 1979.

78. Cole JO, Hartmann E, Brigham P: L-tryptophan: Clinical studies. McLean Hosp J 5:37–71, 1980.

79. Van Praag H, de Haan S: Depression vulnerability and 5-hydroxytryptophan prophylaxis. Psychiatry Res 3:75–83, 1980.

80. Post RM, Goodwin FK: Approaches to brain amines in psychiatric patients: A reevaluation of cerebrospinal fluid studies, in Handbook of Psychopharmacology, Vol. 13.

Edited by Iversen LL, Iversen SD, Snyder SH. Plenum Press, New York, 1978, pp 147–185.

81. Angrist B, Gershon S: Variable attenuation of amphetamine effects by lithium. Am J Psychiatry 136:806–810, 1979.

82. Angrist B, Shopsin B, Gershon S, et al: Metabolites of monoamines in urine and cerebrospinal fluid after large-dose amphetamine administration. Psychopharmacologia 26:1–9, 1972.

83. Ellinwood EH Jr, Sudilowsky A, Nelson L: Behavioral analysis of chronic amphetamine intoxication. Biol Psychiatry 4:215–230, 1972.

84. Watson R, Hartmann E, Schildkraut JJ: Amphetamine withdrawal: Affective state, sleep patterns, and MHPG excretion. Am J Psychiatry 129:263–269, 1972.

85. General Practitioner Research Group: Report 51: Dexamphetamine compared with an inactive placebo in depression. Practitioner 192:151–154, 1964.

86. Van Kammen DP, Murphy DL: Prediction of imipramine antidepressant response by a one-day d-amphetamine trial. Am J Psychiatry 135:1179–1184, 1978.

87. Corsini GU, Del Zompo M, Manconi S, et al: Sedative, hypnotic, and antipsychotic effects of low doses of apomorphine in man, in Advances in Biochemical Pharmacology, Vol. 16. Edited by Costa E, Gessa GL. Raven Press, New York, 1977, pp 645–648.

88. Brown WA, Mueller B: Alleviation of manic symptoms with catecholamine agonists. Am J Psychiatry 136:230–231, 1979.

89. Del Zompo M, Pitzalis GF, Bernardi F, et al: Antipsychotic effect of apomorphine: A retrospective study, in Apomorphine and Other Dopaminomimetics, Vol. 2:

Clinical Pharmacology. Edited by Corsini GU, Gessa GL. Raven Press, New York, 1981, pp 65–76.

90. Jouvent R, Lecrubier Y, Peuch AJ, et al: Antimanic effect of clonidine. Am J Psychiatry 137:1275–1276, 1980.

91. Janowsky DS, El-Yousef MK, Davis JM, et al: Parasympathetic suppression of manic symptoms by physostigmine. Arch Gen Psychiatry 28:542–547, 1973.

92. Davis KL, Berger PA: Pharmacological investigations of the cholinergic imbalance hypothesis of movement disorders and psychosis. Biol Psychiatry 13:23–49, 1978.

93. Cohen BM, Lipinski JF, Altesman RI: Lecithin in the treatment of mania: Double-blind, placebo-controlled trials. Am J Psychiatry 139:1162–1164, 1982.

94. Murphy DL, Campbell I, Costa JL: Current status of the indoleamine hypothesis of the affective disorders, in Psychopharmacology: A Generation of Progress. Edited by Lipton MA, DiMascio A, Killam KF. Raven Press, New York, 1978, pp. 1235–1247.

95. Schatzberg AF, Orsulak PJ, Rosenbaum AH, et al: Toward a biochemical classification of depressive disorders, V: Heterogeneity of unipolar depressions. Am J Psychiatry 139:471–475, 1982.

96. Goodwin FK, Cowdry RW, Webster MH: Predictors of drug response in the affective disorders: Toward an integrated approach, in Psychopharmacology: A Generation of Progress. Edited by Lipton MA, DiMascio A, Killam KF. Raven Press, New York, 1978, pp 1277–1288.

97. Spiker DG, Edwards D, Hanin I, et al: Urinary MHPG and clinical response to amitriptyline in depressed patients. Am J. Psychiatry 137:1183–1187, 1980.

98. Hollister, LE, Davis KL, Berger PA: Subtypes of depression based on excretion of MHPG and response

to nortriptyline. Arch Gen Psychiatry 37:1107–1110, 1980.

99. Schatzberg AF, Rosenbaum AH, Orsulak PJ, et al: Toward a biochemical classification of depressive disorders, III: Pretreatment urinary MHPG levels as predictors of response to treatment with maprotiline. Psychopharmacology 75:34–38, 1981.

100. Schatzberg AF, Rosenbaum AH: Studies on MHPG levels as predictors of antidepressant response. McLean Hosp J 6:138–157, 1981.

101. Hollister LE, Davis KL, Overall JE: Excretion of MHPG in normal subjects: Implications for biological classification of affective disorders. Arch Gen Psychiatry 35:1410–1415, 1978.

102. Wehr TA, Muscettola G, Goodwin FK: Urinary 3-methoxy-4-hydroxyphenylglycol circadian rhythm: Early timing (phase-advance) in manic-depressives compared with normal subjects. Arch Gen Psychiatry 37:257–263, 1980.

103. Blombery PA, Kopin IJ, Gordon EK, et al: Conversion of MHPG to vanillylmandelic acid: Implications for the importance of urinary MHPG. Arch Gen Psychiatry 37:1095–1098, 1980.

104. Maas J: Biogenic amines and depression: Biochemical and pharmacological separation of two types of depression. Arch Gen Psychiatry 32:1357–1361, 1975.

105. García-Sevilla J, Zis AP, Hollingsworth PJ, et al: Platelet α_2-adrenergic receptors in major depressive disorders. Arch Gen Psychiatry 38:1327–1333, 1981.

106. Lerer B, Ebstein RP, Belmaker RH: Subsensitivity of human β-adrenergic adenylate cyclase after salbutamol treatment of depression. Psychopharmacology 75:169–172, 1981.

107. Cohen RM, Campbell IC, Cohen MR, et al: Presynaptic noradrenergic regulation during depression and antidepressant treatment. Psychiatry Res 3:93–105, 1980.
108. Charney DS, Heninger GR, Sternberg DE, et al: Presynaptic adrenergic receptor sensitivity in depression. Arch Gen Psychiatry 38:1334–1340, 1981.
109. Meltzer HY, Arora RC, Baber R, Tricou BJ: Serotonin uptake in blood platelets of psychiatric patients. Arch Gen Psychiatry 38:1322–1326, 1981.
110. Paul SM, Rehavi M, Skolnik P, et al: Depressed patients have decreased binding of tritiated imipramine to platelet serotonin transporter. Arch Gen Psychiatry 38:1315–1317, 1981.
111. Sachar EJ: Neuroendocrine dysfunction in depressive illness. Ann Rev Med 27:389–396, 1976.
112. Ettigi PG, Brown GM: Psychoneuroendocrinology of affective disorder: An overview. Am J Psychiatry 134:493–501, 1977.
113. Prange AJ Jr, Lipton MA, Nemeroff CB, et al: The role of hormones in depression. Life Sciences 20:1305–1318, 1977.
114. Carroll BJ, Feinberg M, Greden JF, et al: A specific laboratory test for the diagnosis of melancholia. Arch Gen Psychiatry 38:15–22, 1981.
115. Carroll BJ: Implications of biological research for the diagnosis of depression, in New Advances in the Diagnosis and Treatment of Depressive Illness. Edited by Mendelwicz J. Elsevier, Amsterdam, 1981, pp 85–107.
116. Sachar EJ, Hellman L, Roffwarg H, et al: Disrupted 24-hour patterns of cortisol secretion in psychotic depression. Arch Gen Psychiatry 28:19–24, 1973.
117. Carroll BJ: Limbic system-adrenal cortex regulation in

depression and schizophrenia. Psychosom Med 38:106–121, 1976.

118. Carroll BJ, Curtis GC, Mendels J: Neuroendocrine regulation in depression. Arch Gen Psychiatry 33:1039–1058, 1976.

119. Rush AJ, Giles DE, Roffwarg HP, Parker CR: Sleep EEG and dexamethasone suppression test findings in outpatients with unipolar major depressive disorders. Biol Psychiatry 17:327–342, 1982.

120. Asnis GM, Sachar EJ, Halbreich U, et al: Cortisol secretion and dexamethasone response in depression. Am J Psychiatry 138:1218–1221, 1981.

121. Davis KL, Hollister LE, Mathé AA, et al: Neuroendocrine and neurochemical measurements in depression. Am J Psychiatry 138:1555–1562, 1981.

122. Fang VS, Tricou BJ, Robertson A, Meltzer HY. Plasma ACTH and cortisol levels in depressed patients: Relation to dexamethasone suppression test. Life Sciences 29:931–938, 1981.

123. Targum SD, Sullivan AC, Byrnes SM: Neuroendocrine interrelationships in major depressive disorder. Am J Psychiatry 139:282–286, 1982.

124. Winokur A, Amsterdam J, Caroff S, et al: Variability of hormonal responses to a series of neuroendocrine challenges in depressed patients. Am J Psychiatry 139:39–44, 1982.

125. Poznanski EO, Carroll BJ, Banegas MC, et al: The dexamethasone suppression test in prepubertal depressed children. Am J Psychiatry 139:321–324, 1982.

126. Spar JE, Gerner R: Does the dexamethasone suppression test distinguish dementia from depression? Am J Psychiatry 139:238–240, 1982.

127. Schlesser MA, Winokur G, Sherman BM: Hypothal-

amic-pituitary-adrenal axis activity in depressive illness. Arch Gen Psychiatry 37:737–743, 1980.

128. Coryell W, Gaffney G, Burkhardt PE: The dexamethasone suppression test and familial subtypes of depression—A naturalistic replication. Biol Psychiatry 17:33–48, 1982.

129. Brown WA, Shuey I: Response to dexamethasone and subtype of depression. Arch Gen Psychiatry 37:747–751, 1980.

130. Nuller JL, Ostroumova MN: Resistance to inhibiting effect of dexamethasone in patients with endogenous depression. Acta Psychiat Scand 61:169–177, 1980.

131. Reus VI, Joseph MS, Dallman MF: ACTH levels after the dexamethasone suppression test in depression. New Engl J Med 306:238–239, 1982.

132. Goldberg IK: Dexamethasone suppression test as indicator of safe withdrawal of antidepressant therapy. Lancet 1:376, 1980.

133. Greden JF, Albala AA, Haskett RF, et al: Normalization of dexamethasone suppression test: A laboratory index of recovery from endogenous depression. Biol Psychiatry 15:449–458, 1980.

134. Halbreich U, Sachar EJ, Asnis GM, et al: Growth hormone responses to dextroamphetamine in depressed patients and normal subjects. Arch Gen Psychiatry 39:189–192, 1982.

135. Loosen PT, Prange AJ Jr: Serum thyrotropin response to thyrotropin-releasing hormone in psychiatric patients: A review. Am J Psychiatry 139:405–416, 1982.

136. Bjørum N, Kirkegaard C: Thyrotropin-releasing-hormone test in unipolar and bipolar depression. Lancet 2:694, 1979.

137. Gold MS, Pottash ALC, Ryan N, et al: TRH-induced TSH response in unipolar, bipolar, and secondary depressions: Possible utility in clinical assessment and differential diagnosis. Psychoneuroendocrinology 5:147–155, 1980.

138. Extein I, Pottash ALC, Gold MS, et al: Differentiating mania from schizophrenia by the TRH test. Am J Psychiatry 137:981–982, 1980.

139. Asnis GM, Nathan RS, Halbreich U, et al: TRH tests in depression. Lancet 1:424–425, 1980.

140. Extein I, Pottash ALC, Gold MS: The thyrotropin-releasing hormone test in the diagnosis of unipolar depression. Psychiatry Res 5:311–316, 1981.

141. Extein I, Pottash ALC, Gold MS, Cowdry RW: Using the protirelin test to distinguish mania from schizophrenia. Arch Gen Psychiatry 39:77–81, 1982.

142. Goodwin FK, Prange AJ, Post RM, et al: Potentiation of antidepressant effects by L-triiodothyronine in tricyclic nonresponders. Am J Psychiatry 139:34–38, 1982.

143. Gold MS, Pottash ALC, Martin DA, et al: Opiate-endorphin test dysfunction in major depression. Neuroscience Abstracts 6:759, 1980.

144. Mendelwicz J, VanCauter E, Linkowski P, et al: The 24-hour profile of prolactin in depression. Life Science 27:2015–2024, 1980.

145. Kupfer DJ, Foster FG: Interval between onset of sleep and rapid eye movement sleep as an indicator of depression. Lancet 2:684–686, 1972.

146. Kupfer DJ, Foster FG, Coble P, et al: The application of EEG sleep for the differential diagnosis of affective disorders. Am J Psychiatry 135:69–74, 1978.

147. Gillin JC, Duncan W, Pettigrew KD, et al: Successful

separation of depressed, normal, and insomniac subjects by EEG sleep data. Arch Gen Psychiatry 36:85–90, 1979.

148. Kupfer DJ, Foster FG, Reich L, et al: EEG sleep changes as predictors in depression. Am J Psychiatry 133:622–626, 1976.

149. Kupfer DJ, Spiker DG, Coble P, et al: EEG sleep and affective disorders: What can it predict? in Catecholamines: Basic and Clinical Frontiers, Vol. 2. Edited by Usdin E, Kopin, IJ, Barchas J. Pergamon Press, New York, 1979, pp 1920–1922.

150. Gillin JC, Wyatt RJ, Fram D, et al: The relationship between changes in REM sleep and clinical improvement in depressed patients treated with amitriptyline. Psychopharmacology 59:267–272, 1978.

151. Vogel GW, Vogel F, McAbee RS, et al: Improvement of depression by REM sleep deprivation. Arch Gen Psychiatry 37:247–253, 1980.

152. Schilgen B, Tölle R: Partial sleep deprivation as therapy for depression. Arch Gen Psychiatry 37:267–271, 1980.

153. Buchsbaum M, Landau S, Murphy D, et al: Average evoked response in bipolar and unipolar affective disorders: Relationship to sex, age of onset, and monoamine oxidase. Biol Psychiatry 7:199–212, 1973.

154. Simpson GM, White KL, Boyd JL, et al: Relationships between plasma antidepressant levels and clinical outcome for inpatients receiving imipramine. Am J Psychiatry 139:358–360, 1982.

155. Cooper TB, Simpson GM, Lee TH: Thymoleptic and neuroleptic drug plasma levels in psychiatry: Current status. Int Rev Neurobiol 19:269–309, 1976.

156. Baldessarini RJ: Status of psychotropic drug blood level

assays and other biochemical measurements in clinical practice. Am J Psychiatry 136:1177–1180, 1979.

157. Risch SC, Janowsky DS, Huey LY: Plasma levels of tricyclic antidepressants and clinical efficacy, in Antidepressants: Neurochemical, Behavioral, and Clinical Perspectives. Edited by Enna SJ, Malick JB, Richelson E. Raven Press, New York, 1981, pp 183–217.

158. Cooper TB, Simpson GM: Prediction of individual dosage of nortriptyline. Am J Psychiatry 135:333–335, 1978.

159. Brunswick DJ, Amsterdam JD, Mendels J, Stern SL: Prediction of steady-state imipramine and desmethylimipramine plasma concentrations from single-dose data. Clin Pharmacol Ther 25:605–610, 1979.

160. Potter WZ, Zavadil AP III, Kopin IJ, et al: Single-dose kinetics predict steady-state concentrations of imipramine and desipramine. Arch Gen Psychiatry 37:314–320, 1980.

161. Murphy DL, Brand E, Goldman T, et al: Platelet and plasma amine oxidase inhibition and urinary amine excretion changes during phenelzine treatment. J Nerv Ment Dis 164:129–134, 1977.

162. Robinson DS, Nies A, Ravaris CL, et al: Clinical pharmacology of phenelzine. Arch Gen Psychiatry 35:629–635, 1978.

163. Giller E Jr, Lieb J: MAO inhibitors and platelet MAO inhibition. Comm Psychopharmacol 4:79–82, 1980.

164. Prange AJ Jr, McCurdy RL, Cochrane CM: The systolic blood pressure response of depressed patients to infused norepinephrine. J Psychiat Res 5:1–13, 1967.

165. Friedman MJ: Does receptor supersensitivity accompany depressive illness? Am J Psychiatry 135:107–109, 1978.

166. Pandey GN, Dysken MW, Garver DL, et al: Beta ad-

renergic receptor function in affective illness. Am J Psychiatry 136:675–678, 1979.

167. Extein I, Tallman J, Smith CC, et al: Changes in lymphocyte beta-adrenergic receptors in depression and mania. Psychiatry Res 1:191–197, 1979.

168. Briley MS, Langer SZ, Raisman R, et al: Tritiated imipramine binding sites are decreased in platelets of untreated depressed patients. Science 209:303–305, 1980.

169. Ramsey TA, Frazer A, Dyson WL, et al: Intracellular lithium and clinical response. Br J Psychiatry 128:103–104, 1976.

170. Pandey GN, Dorus E, Davis JM, et al: Lithium transport in human red blood cells. Arch Gen Psychiatry 36:902–908, 1979.

171. Cohen B, Aoba A: Lithium transport in erythrocytes of manic-depressives (unpublished observations, 1981).

172. Coppen A: Mineral metabolism in affective disorders. Br J Psychiatry 111:1133–1142, 1965.

173. Wehr TA, Wirz-Justice A, Duncan W, et al: Phase advance of the circadian sleep-waking cycle as an antidepressant. Science 206:710–713, 1979.

174. Mathew RJ, Meyer JS, Francis DJ, et al: Cerebral blood flow in depression. Am J Psychiatry 137:1449–1450, 1980.

175. Pearlson GD, Veroff AE, McHugh PR: The use of computed tomography in psychiatry: Recent application to schizophrenia, manic-depressive illness, and dementia syndromes. Johns Hopkins Med J 149:194–202, 1981.

176. Buchsbaum MS, Ingvar DH, Kessler R, et al: Cerebral glucography with positron emission tomography. Arch Gen Psychiatry 39:251–259, 1982.

177. Phelps ME, Mazziotta JC, Kuhl DE, et al: Metabolic mapping of the visual cortex with and without visual

stimulation in volunteers and patients with visual deficits. Neurology 30:432, 1980.

178. Brownell GL, Budinger TF, Lautervur PC, McGeer PL: Positron tomography and nuclear magnetic resonance imaging. Science 215:619–626, 1982.

179. Baldessarini RJ: Biomedical aspects of mood disorders. McLean Hospital J 6:1–34, 1981.

180. Baldessarini RJ: Overview of recent advances in antidepressant pharmacology. McLean Hospital J 7:1–27, 1982.

181. Lovacs M, Beck AT: Maladaptive cognitive structures in depression. Am J Psychiatry 135:1261–1268, 1979.

182. Weissman MM: The psychological treatment of depression. Arch Gen Psychiatry 36:1261–1268, 1979.

183. Akiskal IIS: External validating criteria for psychiatric diagnosis: Their application in affective disorders. J Clin Psychiatry 41(12, Section 2):6–15, 1980.

184. Neborsky RJ, Janowsky DS, Fann WE: Psychopharmacologic and psychotherapeutic interventions: An integrated treatment approach to depression. Psychiat Ann 10:369–380, 1980.

185. Feigner JP: Pharmacology: New antidepressants. Psychiat Ann 10:388–395, 1980.

186. Sulser F: Pharmacology: Current antidepressants. Psychiat Ann 10:381–387, 1980.

187. Shopsin B: Second-generation antidepressants. J Clin Psychiatry 41(12, Section 2):45–46, 1980.

188. Davis JM, Vogel C: Efficacy of trazodone: Data from European and United States studies. J Clin Psychopharmacol 1:27S–34S, 1981.

189. Riblet LA, Taylor DP: Pharmacology and neurochemistry of trazodone. J Clin Psychopharmacol 1:17S–22S, 1981.

151

190. Randrup A, Braestrup C: Uptake inhibition of biogenic amines by newer antidepressant drugs: Relevance to the dopamine hypothesis of depression. Psychopharmacology 53:309–314, 1977.

191. Coupet J, Rauh CE, Szues-Myers VA, Yunger LM: Amoxapine, an antidepressant with antipsychotic properties—A possible role for 7-hydroxyamoxapine. Biochem Pharmacol 28:2514–2515, 1979.

192. Møller-Nielsen I: Tricyclic antidepressants: General pharmacology, in Psychotropic Agents: Antipsychotics and Antidepressants, Vol. 55, Part I, Handbook of Experimental Pharmacology. Edited by Hoffmeister F, Stille G. Berlin, Springer-Verlag, 1980, pp 399–410.

193. Sulser F, Mobley PL: Biochemical effects of antidepressants in animals, in Psychotropic Agents: Antipsychotics and Antidepressants, Vol. 55, Part I, Handbook of Experimental Pharmacology, Edited by Hoffmeister F, Stille G. Berlin, Springer-Verlag, 1980, pp 471–490.

194. Clements-Jewery S, Robson PA, Chidley LJ: Biochemical investigations into the mode of action of trazodone. Neuropharmacology 19:1165–1173, 1980.

195. Fuller RW: Enhancement of monoaminergic neurotransmission by antidepressant drugs, in Antidepressants: Neurochemical, Behavioral, and Clinical Perspectives. Edited by Enna SJ, Malick JB, Richelson E. New York, Raven Press, 1981, pp 1–12.

196. Ban TA: Amoxapine and viloxazine: Review of literature with special reference to clinical studies. Psychopharmacology Bull 15:22–25, 1979.

197. Murphy DL, Lipper S, Campbell IC, et al: Comparative studies of MAO-A and MAO-B inhibitors in man, in Monoamine Oxidase: Structure, Function, and Al-

tered Functions. Edited by Singer TP, VonKorff RW, Murphy DL. New York, Academic Press, 1979, pp 457–475.

198. Maxwell RA, White HL: Tricyclic and monoamine oxidase inhibitor antidepressants: Structure-activity relationships, in Handbook of Psychopharmacology, Vol. 14. Edited by Iversen LL, Iversen SD, Snyder SH. New York, Plenum Press, 1978, pp 83–155.

199. Mendis N, Pare CMB, Sandler M, et al: Is the failure of (−)deprenyl, a selective monoamine oxidase B inhibitor, to alleviate depression related to freedom from the cheese effect? Psychopharmacology 73:87–90, 1981.

200. Morris JB, Beck AT: The efficacy of antidepressant drugs. Arch Gen Psychiatry 30:667–674, 1974.

201. Rogers SC, Clay PM: A statistical review of controlled studies of imipramine and placebo in the treatment of depressive illnesses. Br J Psychiatry 127:599–603, 1975.

202. Kupfer DJ, Detre TP: Tricyclic and monoamine-oxidase-inhibitor antidepressants: Clinical use, in Handbook of Pharmacology, Vol. 14. Edited by Iversen LL, Iversen SD, Snyder SH. New York, Plenum Press, 1978, pp 199–232.

203. Shopsin B, Cassano GB, Conti L: An overview of new "second-generation" antidepressant compounds: Research and treatment implications, in Antidepressants: Neurochemical, Behavioral, and Clinical Perspectives. Edited by Enna SJ, Malick JB, Richelson E. Raven Press, New York, 1981, pp 219–251.

204. Lydiard RB, Gelenberg AJ: Amoxapine—An antidepressant with neuroleptic properties? Pharmacotherapy 1:163–178, 1981.

205. Pinder RM, Brogden RN, Speight TM, Avery GS: Ma-

protiline: A review of its pharmacologic properties and therapeutic efficacy in mental depressive states. Drugs 13:321–352, 1977.

206. Wells BG, Gelenberg AJ: Evaluation of maprotiline hydrochloride. Pharmacotherapy 1:121–139, 1981.

207. Montgomery SA: Review of antidepressant efficacy in inpatients. Neuropharmacology 19:1185–1190, 1980.

208. Settle EC Jr, Ayd FJ Jr: Trimipramine: Twenty years' worldwide clinical experience. J Clin Psychiatry 41:266–274, 1980.

209. Richels K, Chung HR, Csanalosi I, et al: Iprindole and imipramine in non-psychotic depressed out-patients. Br J Psychiatry 123:329–339, 1973.

210. Burgess CD, Turner P: Cardiotoxicity of antidepressant drugs. Neuropharmacology 19:1195–1199, 1980.

211. Smith RC, Chojnacki M, Hu R, Mann E: Cardiovascular effects of therapeutic doses of tricyclic antidepressants: Importance of blood level monitoring. J Clin Psychiatry 41(12, Section 2):57–63, 1980.

212. Axelrod J, Whitby LG, Hertting G: Effect of psychotropic drugs on the uptake of H^3-norepinephrine by tissues. Science 133:383–384, 1961.

213. Cohen BJ, Harris PQ, Altesman RI, Cole JO: Amoxapine: A neuroleptic as well as an antidepressant? Am J Psychiatry 139:1165–1167, 1982.

214. Oates JA, Fann WE, Cavanaugh JH: Effect of doxepin on the norepinephrine pump: A preliminary report. Psychosomatics 10(3, Section 2):12–13, 1969.

215. Stewart RM, Campbell A, Sperk G, Baldessarini RJ: Receptor mechanisms in increased sensitivity to serotonin agonists after dihydroxytryptamine shown by electronic monitoring of muscle twitches in the rat. Psychopharmacology 60:281–289, 1979.

216. Peroutka SJ, Snyder SH: Long-term antidepressant treatment decreases spiroperidol-labeled serotonin receptor binding. Science 210:88–90, 1980.

217. Peroutka SJ, Snyder SH: Interactions of antidepressants with neurotransmitter receptor sites, in Antidepressants: Neurochemical, Behavioral, and Clinical Perspectives. Edited by Enna SJ, Malick JB, Richelson E. New York, Raven Press, 1981, pp 75–90.

218. Richelson E, Divenetz-Romero S: Blockade by psychotropic drugs of the muscarinic acetylcholine receptor in cultured nerve cells. Biol Psychiatry 12:771–785, 1977.

219. Richelson E: Tricyclic antidepressants: Interactions with histamine and muscarinic acetylcholine receptors, in Antidepressants: Neurochemical, Behavioral, and Clinical Perspectives. Edited by Enna SJ, Malick JB, Richelson E. New York, Raven Press, 1981, pp 53–73.

220. Kanof PD, Greengard P: Brain histamine receptors as targets for antidepressant drugs. Nature 272:329–333, 1978.

221. Paul SM, Rehavi M, Pice K, et al: Does high-affinity [^{3}H]imipramine binding label serotonin reuptake sites in brain and platelet? Life Sciences 28:2253–2260, 1981.

222. Kendall DA, Stancel GM, Enna SJ: The influence of sex hormones on antidepressant-induced alterations in neurotransmitter receptor binding. J Neuroscience 2:354–360, 1982.

223. Paykel ES: Management of acute depression, in Psychopharmacology of Affective Disorders. Edited by Paykel ES, Coppen A. New York, Oxford University Press, 1979, pp 235–247.

224. Baldessarini RJ: Schizophrenia. New Engl J Med 297:988–995, 1977.

225. Creese I, Burt DR, Snyder SH: Biochemical actions of

neuroleptic drugs: Focus on the dopamine receptor, in Handbook of Psychopharmacology, Vol 10: Neuroleptics and Schizophrenia. Edited by Iversen LL, Iversen SD, Snyder SH. New York, Plenum Press, 1978, pp 37–89.

226. McMillen BA, Warnack W, German DC, Shore PA: Effects of chronic desipramine treatment on rat brain noradrenergic responses to β-adrenergic drugs. Eur J Pharmacol 61:239–246, 1980.

227. Maj J, Mogilnicka E, Klimek V: The effect of repeated administration of antidepressant drugs on the responsiveness of rats to catecholamine agonists. J Neural Transmission 44:221–235, 1979.

228. Menkes DB, Aghajanian GK, McCall RB: Chronic antidepressant treatment enhances α-adrenergic and serotonergic responses in the facial nucleus. Life Sciences 27:45–55, 1980.

229. Rehavi M, Ramot O, Yavetz, B, Sokolovsky M: Amitryptyline: Long-term treatment elevates α-adrenergic and muscarinic receptor binding in mouse brain. Brain Res 194:443–453, 1980.

230. Enna SJ, Mann E, Kendall D, Stancel GM: Effect of chronic antidepressant administration on brain neurotransmitter receptor binding, in Antidepressants: Neurochemical, Behavioral, and Clinical Perspectives. Edited by Enna SJ, Malick JB, Richelson E. New York, Raven Press, 1981, pp 91–105.

231. Sulser F, Vetulani J, Mobley PI: Mode of action of antidepressant drugs. Biochem Pharmacol 27:257–261, 1978.

232. Sellinger-Barnette MM, Mendels J, Frazer A: The effect of psychoactive drugs on beta-adrenergic receptor

binding sites in rat brain. Neuropharmacology 19:447–454, 1980.

233. Crews FT, Paul SM, Goodwin FK: Acceleration of β-receptor desensitization in combined administration of antidepressants and phenoxybenzamine. Nature 290:787–789, 1981.

234. Siggins GR, Schultz JE: Chronic treatment with lithium or desipramine alters discharge frequency and norepinephrine responsiveness of cerebellar Purkinje cells. Proc Natl Acad Sci USA 76:5987–5991, 1979.

235. Olphe HR, Schellenberg A: Reduced sensitivity of neurons to noradrenaline after chronic treatment with antidepressant drugs. Eur J Pharmacol 63:7–13, 1980.

236. Szabadi E: Review: Adrenoreceptors on central neurons: Microiontophoretic studies. Neuropharmacology 18:831–843, 1979.

237. Waal HJ: Propranolol-induced depression. Br Med J 2:50, 1967.

238. Savage DD, Mendels J, Frazer A. Monoamine oxidase inhibitors and serotonin uptake inhibitors: Differential effects on [^{3}H]serotonin binding sites in rat brain. J Pharmacol Exp Ther 212:259–263, 1980.

239. Serra G, Argiolas A, Klimek V, et al: Chronic treatment with antidepressants prevents the inhibitory effect of small doses of apomorphine on dopamine synthesis and motor activity. Life Sciences 25:415–424, 1979.

240. Charney DS, Menkes DB, Henninger GR: Receptor sensitivity and the mechanism of action of antidepressant treatment. Arch Gen Psychiatry 38:1160–1180, 1981.

241. Chiodo L, Antelman SM: Repeated tricyclics induce a

progressive dopamine autoreceptor subsensitivity independent of daily drug treatment. Nature 287:451–454,
1980.

242. Chiodo L, Antelman SM: Electroconvulsive shock:
Progressive dopamine autoreceptor subsensitivity independent of repeated treatment. Science 210:799–801,
1980.

243. Deakin JFW, Owen F, Cross AJ, Dashwood MJ: Studies on possible mechanisms of action of electroconvulsive therapy: Effects of repeated electrically induced
seizures on rat brain receptors for monoamines and
other neurotransmitters. Psychopharmacology 73:345–
349, 1981.

244. Wielosz M: Increased sensitivity to dopaminergic agonists after repeated electroconvulsive shock (ECS) in
rats. Neuropharmacology 20:941–945, 1981.

245. Asakura M, Tsukamoto T, Hasegawa K: Modulation of
rat brain α_2 and β-adrenergic receptor sensitivity following long-term treatment with antidepressants. Brain
Res 235:192–197, 1982.

246. Maggi A, U'Prichard DC, Enna SJ: Differential effects
of antidepressant treatment on brain monoaminergic
receptors. Eur J Pharmacol 61:91–98, 1980.

247. Friedman E, Dallob A: Enhanced serotonin receptor
activity after chronic treatment with imipramine or
amitriptyline. Commun Psychopharmacol 3:89–92,
1979.

248. Mogilnicka E, Klimek V: Mianserin, danitracen, and
amitryptyline withdrawal increases the behavioral responses of rats to L-5HTP. J Pharm Pharmacol 31:704–
705, 1979.

249. Gallager DW, Bunney WE Jr: Failure of chronic lith-

ium treatment to block tricyclic antidepressant-induced 5HT supersensitivity. Naunyn-Schmiedeberg's Arch Pharmacol 307:129–133, 1979.

250. Jones RSG: Enhancement of 5-hydroxytryptamine-induced behavioral effects following chronic administration of antidepressant drugs. Psychopharmacology 69:307–311, 1980.

251. Fibiger HC, Phillips AG: Increased intracranial self-stimulation in rats after long-term administration of desipramine. Science 214:683–685, 1981.

252. McGuire PS, Seiden LS: The effects of tricyclic antidepressants on performance under a differential-reinforcement-of-low-rates schedule in rats. J Pharmacol Exp Ther 214:635–641, 1980.

253. Kinnier WJ, Chuang D-M, Gwynn G, Costa E: Characteristics and regulation of high-affinity [³II]imipramine binding to rat hippocampal membranes. Neuropharmacology 20:411–419, 1981.

254. Sette M, Raisman R, Briley M, Langer SZ: Localization of tricyclic antidepressant binding sites on serotonin nerve terminals. J Neurochem 37:40–42, 1981.

255. Lee C-M, Snyder SH: Norepinephrine neuronal uptake binding sites in rat brain membranes labeled with [³H]desipramine. Proc Natl Acad Sci USA 78:5250–5254, 1981.

256. Bielski RJ, Friedel RD: Prediction of tricyclic antidepressant response. Arch Gen Psychiatry 33:1479–1489, 1976.

257. Coppen A, Ghose K, Montgomery S, et al: Continuation therapy with amitriptyline in depression. Br J Psychiatry 133:28–33, 1978.

258. Prien RF: Continuation therapy in depression: Obser-

vations from a multihospital study. Presented at the annual meeting of the American College of Neuropsychopharmacology, San Juan, PR, December 1980.

259. Bialos D, Giller E, Jatlow P, et al: Recurrence of depression after the discontinuation of long-term amitriptyline treatment. Am J Psychiatry 139:325–329, 1982.

LIST OF
ABBREVIATIONS

Acetyl-CoA	acetyl-coenzyme-A
ACh	acetylcholine
AChE	acetylcholinesterase
ACTH	adrenocorticotropic hormone
AER	average evoked response
AMPT	α-methylparatyrosine
ATP	adenosine-triphosphate
BP	bipolar (bipolar or manic depressive disorder)
CA	catecholamine
CAT	choline-acetyl transferase
CNS	central nervous system
COMT	catechol-O-methyl transferase
CRF	corticotropin-releasing factor
CSF	cerebrospinal fluid
cyclic-AMP	3',5'-cyclic-adenosine-monophosphate
DA	dopamine
DBH	dopamine-β-hydroxylase
DOPA	dihydroxyphenylamine

LIST OF ABBREVIATIONS

DST	dexamethasone suppression test
DZ	dizygotic
ECT	electroconvulsive therapy
EEG	electroencephalographic
FSH	follicle-stimulating hormone
GH	growth hormone
GMP	guanosine monophosphate
GnRH	gonadotropin-releasing hormone
HCA	heterocyclic antidepressant
HVA	homovanillic acid
ITT	insulin-tolerance test
LH	luteinizing hormone
LSD	lysergic acid diethylamide
MAO	monoamine oxidase
MHPG	3-methoxy-4-hydroxyphenethyleneglycol
MZ	monozygotic
NE	norepinephrine
PCPA	para-chlorophenylalanine
PL	prolactin
REM	rapid-eye-movement (sleep)
S-AMe	S-adenosylmethionine
TRH	thyrotropin-releasing hormone

Try	L-tryptophan
TSH	thyroid-stimulating hormone
UP	unipolar (major depression)
VMA	vanillylmandelic acid
³H-QNB	[³H]-quinuclidinyl benzilate
5-HIAA	5-hydroxyindoleacetic acid
5-HT	5-hydroxytryptamine
5-HTP	5-hydroxytryptophan
6-OHDA	6-hydroxydopamine